The GIFT of JOB LOSS

The GIFT of JOB LOSS

A Practical Guide to Realizing the Most Rewarding Time of Your Life

MICHAEL FROEHLS, Ph.D.

Peitho Publishing

Editorial Production: Sharon Lindenburger, Joanne Sprott

Book Design: Lori S. Malkin

Photo credits:
© Daniel Grill | Tetra Image / Corbis
© Dejan Sarman | Dreamstime.com
© Jan Matoška | Dreamstime.com

Library of Congress Control Number: 2010941358

Includes bibliographical references and index.

ISBN 978-0-9831192-0-3 (paperback)

THE GIFT OF JOB LOSS website: **www.thegiftofjobloss.com**.

. . . .

BULK ORDER INFORMATION

If you are a corporation, outplacement firm, college, university, or any other organization interested in purchasing larger quantities of this book at a discount, please write to Peitho Publishing, 54 Rainey Street, Suite 718, Austin, Texas 78701, or send an email to **bulksales@peithopublishing.com**. Generous quantity discounts are available for educational purposes, fund-raising, and gift-giving.

For all hard-working employees
facing job loss now or
later in life

PREFACE

This book on "job loss" is very different from everything you have likely read on this subject. This is not your typical career book.

The Gift of Job Loss does not tell you how to find a job. It does not offer you legal advice on how to maximize severance payments. You will not find advice on how to network, write a cover letter, or master your job interview skills. Neither is this a "get rich quick" book nor an "escape" book to wherever.

So, what is this book really about and why should you read it?

The book's mission is to overcome your fear of job loss and the negativity surrounding such a highly charged topic in this difficult economy. Instead of being paralyzed by fear or discouraged by the seeming dearth of new job opportunities, I want you to see the incredible, mostly overlooked, never talked about and completely forgotten upside that your new situation offers.

I call it the "gift of job loss." It is a gift, because this new situation is handed to you; it is not your own making. It is a gift, because your job loss carries a lot of good things, like an unopened present under the Holiday tree. This great gift is the gift of time. All of a sudden you have time on your hands, time you can use strategically to build your future, to catch up with the past, or whatever you decide to do with it. This is time you have probably never had in years, if not decades, of hard work during employment. Once you realize that your time, in fact your lifetime, is your most important commodity, you will start seeing job loss in a different, more positive light.

My goal is to help you analyze your individual situation, and then make a decision about how to use your time. Factors influencing your own decision are your personal needs, potential mental and real constraints, and the economic situation around you. I will help guide you to come up with a plan that is an alternative to going right into a frantic job search—your natural reflexive response to job loss. This is an opportunity for you to reflect, plan, and dream about taking one, three, or even six months off to pursue a diverse set of activities that might never occur again in your life—activities that might ultimately make you happier, healthier, and even richer than trying to find a job immediately.

It is likely that many important things in life for you have often been, by choice or by necessity, your second priority behind work. Examples are: not enough quality time with your family; never having enjoyed a true, uninterrupted and long dream vacation; letting your financial situation slip; postponing life-extending measures such as regular physical exercise or losing weight; or whatever else has been missing in your life that you have been postponing for another day, a day that has never come…until now.

My ideas and actionable advice should change your view about job loss profoundly. People I have talked with about the key ideas in this book have started using them as a guide in their daily life. Just one example: A good friend of mine recently lost her job. She got inspired, reflected on her situation, and decided on some desired activities to pursue before starting her job search. Her pessimism turned into optimism and joy. In order to keep her morale up and for a daily reminder of her plan ahead, she posted her goals and desired activities on her fridge. She admits neither she nor any of her family and colleagues had ever thought about job loss the way this book helped them to view it.

You only live once. Turn job loss into the most rewarding time of your life. Feel free to drop me a note on how this book changed your outlook on job loss and what you decided to do (**michael@thegiftofjobloss.com**).

▩ ▩ ▩

TABLE OF CONTENTS

INTRODUCTION

SEEING THE UPSIDE OF JOB LOSS—A NEW PERSPECTIVE

▦ ▦ ▦

When I set out to take time off after losing my position, I had no intention to write a book about it. My mind was focused on planning and getting the most out of my post-employment time ahead. Contrary to most people facing lay-off, I realized the upside and the gift that job loss can bring. I resisted the urge to get right back into the job market. Job loss would give me time, the real short commodity of our finite lives, time you or I usually don't have during our working days, weeks, months, and years.

After 15 years of working in Strategy Consulting and in Corporate America, and with more than 20 working years ahead until retirement, how wonderful to be given the opportunity, a true gift, to spend time outside work for a while. How wonderful to pursue various activities that either fell through the cracks when working 60 hours a week, or things I could not have accomplished during the short vacation times allocated to an employee in Corporate America. How wonderful to travel to amazing destinations and not worry about whether in the future I might have the health and opportunity to explore them.

I maximized the benefits of the free time without being reckless about it. Everything I did was analyzed and measured as you can expect from a former executive in Corporate America. Instead of panicking, I paused, took stock of my situation, my needs, and the economic and job market situation around me. I looked at the pros and cons of going straight into a job search vs. taking some time to bring my life up to date, investing in some new skills, spending time with family, and traveling to several exciting locations that I had always wanted to see during my lifetime. In other words, I did what many only dream about.

You might think that this is strange, weird, foolhardy, or just crazy. You might think only millionaires can afford to not immediately look for a new job after losing one. Isn't job loss bad? How can job loss possibly be rewarding and beneficial for you?

I hope to convince you that job loss can be an amazing gift for many employees in this country.

I wrote this book because ex-colleagues, headhunters, friends, and business contacts reacted with a mix of admonishment, envy, and acceptance when learning about my approach to my job loss. Their message to me was simple:

> *"Michael, other people can learn from you and your experience. You made an extremely smart move to use your time in the way you did. Most people who are about to or have just lost their job would not come up with the idea of first optimizing their life outside the job search, or if so, would not know how to justify or plan for it. Due to our immense focus on jobs and careers, magnified by our upbringing, and being so scared by perceived and real financial and family needs, many of us would instantly go into job search without any further thought."*

My time of job loss brought me incredible happiness. It gave me relaxation, self-reflection, and immense energy. I gathered new ideas for my career ahead, potential investments, and start-ups. I learned a new language. I increased my knowledge about Latin America, one of the most dynamic growth stories today. Thanks to some amazing travel, I brought home great souvenirs that remind me every day of my year off. Also, my timing of skipping the period of the Great Recession was dead-on as the economic picture looked brighter on my return than when I started my time off.

WHEN JOB SEARCH MEANS LOST OPPORTUNITY

I talked to many people who after losing their jobs had stayed put and desperately tried to find a job. Some of them were depressed, unhappy, pale, and some were even taking medications. They had gone right back into job search. For them, it was a mind thing. They could not disengage from the mental box they were in. They keenly felt the pressure to find the next job immediately.

The most amazing thing was that many could have easily afforded three, six or even twelve months without pursuing new employment. Nobody seemed to be able to look at what is even more precious in our life than money or an income-generating job—our time on this earth. It was rare to find somebody who analyzed what else you could do with your time for a few weeks or months instead of immediately going back into the workplace.

Of those looking for jobs, some had found one after a short while, though often at a grossly lower pay rate. They were already looking for the next job in order to get back to their previous compensation level. Some had been looking for over a year in vain—and I am talking about highly educated people with decent work histories.

Successful in their job search or not, none of them had even considered using the event of job loss to do the once-in-a-lifetime vacation, to wait out the recession, or to use the free time strategically by checking out a different location to live, go back to school, or spend quality time with family.

There is no doubt that in many cases a person's financial situation is dire when job loss happens. Health or family constraints mandate immediate job search or taking on any job available to pay the bills. On the other side and based on my experience, financial concerns or a family is often a pretext to go straight into job search instead of using your time alternatively for a short while. It is often not going to be as dire as you think, if you do take some time off. Going right back into job search can also be a shield to avoid asking yourself potentially uncomfortable questions about priorities in your life, especially job/money vs. personal and family time. A family can be a source of strength and often provides income when one spouse loses employment. Many people have sufficient savings including a potential severance payment to postpone job search by at least a few months. It is their mindset of fear that will cause havoc and does not allow them to make a rational analysis about the trade-off between time and money. They reject the gift of job loss automatically because they cannot rationalize it for themselves or defend it in front of others.

JOB LOSS IS TO BE EXPECTED DURING YOUR LIFE TIME

▨ ▨ ▨

The idea behind the book can be summarized in five points:

1. *You should expect job loss during your working life:* You will work probably between 30 and 40 years total in a lifetime. The chance of losing your job at least once is very high. That risk is totally independent of your level of hierarchy or education or your skills. The risk is also largely independent of your overall performance. If a merger happens, or a restructuring, your boss does not like you, or a cost cutting program eliminates your unit, you are history.

2. *Your lifetime is limited and unknown to you:* While you might expect to live to a certain old age based on actuarial tables, you might be out of luck much earlier. Just look around at your friends and family and see how many have already died or are suffering diseases in their thirties, forties, and fifties. This could be you tomorrow. This means you have to decide whether to optimize your life based on the actuarial tables or play a more risk-averse game, i.e., not waiting until retirement to enjoy life.

3. *Time and money are both scarce and there is a trade-off:* Money is what makes you survive and enjoy life. It takes time to earn money. That is why you work. As a consequence, money and time are both scarce resources and there is a trade-off between the two. Every day spent working will not come back and is lost forever for doing non-work activities like spending time with your kids. It is

difficult to get this trade-off of money and time right, though our work ethic seems to bias our decisions favoring money over time.

4. *Human beings are bad at allocating time strategically:* We have a hard time thinking ahead in years or decades. We either over- or underestimate the effect of time and timing on our career, job, education, investments, and personal life. We fail to see that many things in life are time dependent. And specific opportunities will not come back once a certain point has passed. We might postpone a trip with a family member for career reasons only to see this person pass away "too early."

Taking points 1 through 4 together, leads to the most important one:

5. *Job loss can be an amazing gift—a valuable opportunity as it frees up time: Job loss hands you free time. You have a choice:* At that moment you can go right back into job search and the next job. Or you can accept and explore the valuable option of first pursuing other activities for which you might not have had sufficient time during the previous years of employment, and likely might not have sufficient time for after you start a new job. More precisely, my experience suggests that you can pursue about 7 no-regret activities and up to 8 optional activities that might change your career and life. It is up to you whether you accept the potentially once in lifetime gift and its inherent value, or reject it.

READ THIS BOOK IF YOU FACE JOB LOSS

If you work and are about to lose your job or have just recently lost your employment, you can benefit from this book. You have had probably only between two to four weeks annual vacation time for years, have been struggling with family and work obligations, and are always short of time. You might have worked five, ten, or twenty years already and are starting to regret more and more things you should have done but never did because of lack of time. You have dreams that you have not been able to realize because of lack of time even more than of lack of money.

Now, you are scared about potential or actual job loss. Before you start your job search and sign up for outplacement, or whatever job search-related steps you are about to take, read this book first. It will open your eyes to the upside of job loss, make you feel better and empowered, and help you to find your personal course of action. You cannot change your upcoming or recent job loss, but you can turn this situation into a unique opportunity for your happiness, career, and personal life, an opportunity that might never come back in the future.

The ideas in this book could also be valuable if you are not part of Corporate America. You could be retiring from your service in the military after ten or twenty years and are about to embark on the next phase of your life. You might feel the same initial disorientation like somebody laid off in Corporate America. Leaving public service involuntarily or due to early retirement can have the same effect and puts you in a place not much different from the private sector. I hope that this book helps you in your transition.

MY GOALS: TO HELP YOU MANAGE YOUR JOB LOSS AND REALIZE THE MOST REWARDING TIME OF YOUR LIFE

▨ ▨ ▨

The Gift of Job Loss is a self-help book with all the ingredients you expect—key concepts and underlying rationale, actionable and practical advice for you on what to do when facing job loss, plus a selection of resources you might find useful. While you can read this book in any order you like, following its flow might help you to get the most out of it.

PART I –THE GIFT OF JOB LOSS presents a new perspective on losing your job. We start by discussing the pros and cons of the common wisdom of going straight back into the labor market after job loss. This is often a safe bet from a pure career perspective and supported by a whole industry helping job seekers. We will then talk about the shortcomings of immediately applying for a job and introduce a new perspective. This new perspective views job loss as a gift as it frees up time for you, a gift you can accept or reject. The gift is that instead of going right back into the job market, you have free time now, that you can use to your benefit. You will learn about 15 activities you might choose to follow. They are the key elements of *The Gift of Job Loss* and should help you make the proverbial lemonade out of the lemon of job loss.

PART II –STRATEGIC USE OF TIME AT THE CORE OF THE GIFT. What makes job loss truly a gift? It is the freeing up of time that you usually don't have. This is time you can use strategically for many of the 15 activities, time that you did not have during employment, and time that you won't have again when taking on your next position. Therefore, you should get clarity about the value of time for you, in particular regarding the trade-off with money. You will read about the fundamental issue of optimizing your time on earth, not knowing how long it will last. As human beings, we often have a distorted view about time. Do you expect to make it to old age healthy and lead your life, including your career, based on retirement at 65 in order to live life thereafter? Or do you protect against early death and disease by following a different path including taking some time off after job loss, as advocated here? This section of the book should empower you to deal with time more skillfully. Beyond the concept of lifetime, you will read about the concept of opportunity costs. You will see why taking time off during bad economic times makes economic sense and might be a good strategy. In bad times, you not only use your lifetime wisely, but also the costs of doing so are very low.

PART III –MAKING THE MOST OUT OF YOUR GIFT shares practical advice with you about how to get the most out of your job loss by managing your time off wisely. I am using a Socratic Q&A style to make it easy for you to get answers to 12 common questions. For example, we address issues of optimal length of time off, goal setting, financial planning, potential family constraints, how to stay in contact with the job market, and what to tell others.

A very extensive APPENDIX supplements *Part III* by providing more practical, actionable advice, information, and go-to resources. In *Appendix A*, you will find specific advice on what to do with regard to job loss based on how close you are to it. I provide specific, multi-step recommendations for three distinct situations—first, when you see the proverbial writing on the wall while still being employed; second, what to do and not do right after lay-off; and third, how to prepare for job loss years in advance, in case you bought this book still being "safely" employed.

In *Appendix B,* you can read a primer on severance policies and packages and what you need to know about this great benefit left for you in most of Corporate America.

In *Appendix C,* you will find a short, but meaningful, selection of reading material on each topic that I touch upon in the book. Each of the authors mentioned is worth reading. I recommend that you use *The Gift of Job Loss* as a starting point before digging deeper into the topics and suggested books that are of particular interest to you.

From time to time in the book, you will come across my story of job loss, thoughts, descriptions of my time off, and lastly my conclusions on whether it was worth it in my *Epilogue.* I do this not because I feel special, but to give you some context and make this book more lively. You can use my case as an example for what I am describing or even for inspiration. If you like my anecdotes, you can find some corresponding amazing pictures from my travels on my website: www.thegiftofjobloss.com. Conversely, if you dislike reading personal accounts and just want to focus on the main message, feel free to do so.

Since you made it this far, it is time for two important remarks.

First, deviating from the masses by taking time off and using it in a meaningful way might change you, whether you take three or six months off before applying for your next job or going for your next career move. Time off allows you to think, ask questions, and seek answers you usually would not have the time for. This might be your main risk or rather the greatest chance, if you allow it to happen.

Second, I hope that you are not looking for monetary proof for the underlying thesis of this book. No, your humble author is not a billionaire. Once you understand the main message of this book, though, you will realize that the gift of job loss is not about making millions after your time off. It is not a "get rich quick" book, at least not in the monetary sense. Nor is it about radical change in your life or about escaping Corporate America. *The Gift of Job Loss* is about using your time strategically for a period of your choosing, thereby increasing your well-being, your happiness, and ultimately improving your career and long-term life path.

I hope you make the most out of your job loss! Have courage and enjoy!

Michael A, Froehls, Ph.D.

Part I
The Gift of Job Loss

THE GIFT OF JOB LOSS

From gloom to joy—Embracing job loss

Mirroring the economy at large, 2008 was a bad year for me. I can't recollect another year in the economy, stock market, and job situation where everything seemed to be going downhill in parallel. I was doing great in the aftermath of the dot.com bubble, but this animal, later labeled the deepest economic recession since the 1930s, looked decidedly different.

The company started a huge program to cut costs and reorganize. It became clear that my team, including me, would be at risk. As a former management consultant specializing in performance improvement, I knew how the cost-cutting game would be playing out, what departments would be at risk. Of course, it was all probabilities and I might get lucky, though I had no high hopes.

I had always been a very conservative and diversified investor. It did not help. I lost temporarily over 30% of my net worth. What a disaster! Many people with heavy losses in their portfolio think about how they can make up for them.

For me, this calamity triggered a totally different thought. A quick calculation of how much my losses were in the equivalent of annual income from employment, in terms of time spent working, gave me pause. "Wow, Michael, if you can lose that much in such a short time due to factors largely outside of your control, wouldn't you have been better off spending the money on things that would have made you happy or using the time differently if you had known in advance?" Working full-time usually means you cannot do anything else during that time. Maybe the value of today's time was more important than I was giving it credit for? Why work every year of your life until 65, if savings can disappear so quickly, for whatever reasons, but certain activities can't be done later in life?

While contemplating the value of time and the trade-off with work and money, my thoughts always went back to friends of my age and younger who already had serious health issues. Realizing my own mortality through their woes just added to my gloom.

"Don't push the ocean" is the favorite saying of a friend of mine. What she means is that when things are leaning a certain way, maybe it is for a reason. Instead of going against the tide, ride the wave. Maybe she was right. My brain started to work overtime. A mix of thoughts seemed to come to the surface, not very well aligned, uneven, nagging, and not making too much sense at first. The idea of taking some time off, of not fighting the potential job loss but embracing it with vigor, was slowly nesting in my head. Like a ray of sunlight parting the clouds, my gloom started to dissipate.

While I considered myself lucky with four weeks of "personal days off," this was not a lot since I had to use half of it for family visits overseas. That did not leave time for even a three-week uninterrupted trip to anywhere or for taking two months to learn something new. Making me more depressed was the knowledge that almost every person in Europe has five or six weeks vacation time plus more public holidays than we have in the US. From that perspective, I was eyeing the potential job loss with some curiosity. Job loss means free time without asking anybody for time off. "Work hard, play hard," they say…it was time to focus on the "play hard" part of the equation.

There were plenty of things that I had always postponed because there was never enough time. Learning a new language was on my list that would help me professionally. Visiting some ancient cities I had dreamt of for years was on my agenda. Same goes for spending quality time with my mom and taking her to her birthplace. The ideas just kept coming. I was now, first slowly then increasingly, embracing the expected job loss as the best thing that could ever happen to me. After fifteen years of working in high pressured jobs, the moment was about to come to benefit from what I started to label in my head the gift of job loss, a gift of free time. Where I now saw a once-in-a-lifetime opportunity that presented itself during this economic crisis, many of my coworkers and friends saw the world coming to an end.

On a seemingly normal day in October 2008, I was finally called into my boss's office. It was not entirely unexpected. I had even been thinking about what I would do when I lost my job, and had decided not to panic, but instead to see it as a valuable opportunity for "time off," even though I knew that people would think I was crazy for doing so. I received my 60-day termination notice and a bit later the details of separation.

There was something really interesting about my conversation with my boss. She is a great person and was later let go as well. When I received the papers and mentioned that I was planning to take some time off to travel for a few months, she started moving around in her chair. It was amazing, this accomplished woman with a great family, nice home outside New York, financially well-off, was shaking a bit. I doubt whether she noticed it. Clearly, it was not fathomable to her that somebody had the guts to just kiss the whole economic mess and his own job loss good-bye and take time off. I was not announcing that I would retire on a tropical island and become a surfer dude. I was not complaining about the company, in fact I offered to return for the right opportunity if it ever presented itself. I just said that I would probably take a few months off to travel the world, realize a few things on my "bucket list," and invest in some new language skills.

For her, however, even taking off just a few weeks, as she later proudly told me, was a big, big thing. And needless to say, she found a very good position only a short while later after leaving the company. It was mainly in my conversation with her that I realized for the first time that people are frequently held back not by financial constraints, but by other factors like conformity, fear, or limits they knowingly or unknowingly impose on themselves.

The two-plus months of knowing when the last day in the office would be were kind of strange. The company did not demand daily presence in the office anymore. The economic news was deteriorating, friends got laid off, and New York's winter was arriving.

I spent a lot of time playing the piano, enjoying walking in my neighborhood, and going to the gym frequently. I hired a personal trainer who made me sweat and do things with weights and other machines that I had never dared to try before. This was great. I lost a few pounds, built some muscle. As an extra treat, I met self-employed friends in the early afternoon or late morning when others were at work. It was the perfect transition period. I started shredding years of documents and papers and brought my life up to date. I cleaned up my place more than necessary, threw out old stuff, and gave items to charity.

As an opera buff, I enjoyed my Metropolitan Opera subscription to the fullest. I also started some Spanish classes online, and began to accumulate some information on travel destinations. No more Sundays without going to Barnes and

Noble after the evening service. Time flew by, Christmas came, and I flew home to Europe to spend the holidays with my family. At this point, I knew that I would do some amazing things in 2009 but I had no concrete plans yet. I was in my own little world.

Hiking or being in the air is the moment when I have my best thoughts. The shower also works but it does not beat enjoying a glass of red wine (or two…) over the blue or dark skies over the Atlantic Ocean. What was my situation? What to do next?

Everything looked surprisingly obvious to me. With the economy further sliding, the chances of finding new employment rapidly were slim. In other words, the opportunity costs of not looking for a job aggressively would be close to zero. I would not be missing anything. Even better, I would escape all the negativity around me.

I am all for trying hard and "going all in" as they say in poker, but I was not going to bang on closed doors. After fifteen years of having a successful career, I saw no need to get masochistic and depressed.

I could barely sit calmly in my Economy Class seat because of all the excitement. I took out a pen and paper and the American Airlines world maps from their in-flight magazine. Where could I go? With whom would I travel? When is the best season? It was winter, where to start? What to do first?

How to do all this financially? I felt like a kid in a candy store. Never mind that I would be out of a job in a few days...the gift of job loss was in front of me. I was thanking God for the courage, vision, and the opportunity to do whatever was lying ahead.

Upon landing, I had made my mind up: I was going to take six months off, but was tacitly open to go up to twelve months depending on circumstances. I also decided to move to sunny Austin, the city where I had received my graduate degree almost two decades ago. I had always wanted to return eventually. It seemed that the right moment had arrived to give Texas a closer look. The lower living expenses compared to New York City would be a big plus as well. When I called the movers after my return to the US, they asked me "Michael, what is going on in Austin? Every second quote we are giving this week is related to Austin." I had no answer, but smiled. It was a good omen.

On my last day at the office, I handed back the keys, the laptop, the Blackberry, shredded any remaining papers, walked out on Bryant Park, and looked back a last time at the beautiful new office building I had worked in. A strange mix of anxiety and excitement filled me. The gift of time had finally come.

INTRODUCTION

▦ ▦ ▦

We will begin this section by taking a look at the conventional advice for job seekers of going straight into job search after job loss. Then, we will contrast it with an alternative approach. The conventional advice is usually the safe way to follow if you just want to optimize your working life. Unfortunately, it might not be the best way to optimize your life overall. That's why we will take a close look at a different perspective that I label the "gift of job loss." It offers 15 activities at your disposal when faced with job loss. These consist of 7 no-regret activities and 8 optional activities.

THE BENEFITS OF IMMEDIATE JOB SEARCH

▦ ▦ ▦

You know the usual advice for people who have just lost their jobs. It goes like this:

> *"Take a deep breath and start your job search as soon as possible. It's OK to take a short one or two week break to clear your mind, but don't delay. Your job search will take time, at least three to nine months depending on your seniority. The longer you are out of a job, the harder it will be for you to find one. If you delay for too long, you might even reach the point of no return; you might become long-term unemployed for good. Don't delay. File for unemployment, update your résumé, start networking, and get on with the job search program. If your company pays for outplacement services, use them."*

This is conventional wisdom and most people follow it. On the surface, there is nothing wrong with it, since there is safety in going with the crowd and being "normal." It usually works. Or does it?

Around the time of job loss, people often start buying books on "how to find a job" or "how to write a cover letter." Some may purchase books to help them reassess their strengths and weaknesses. Others venture out and ask the question whether to continue in the current industry or to do something else.

The variety of career-oriented self-help books is amazing and you should find what you are looking for. It can, however, also be a bit overwhelming. Add the pressure from friends, family, and colleagues, financial concerns, and the negative media coverage of how bad the economy is, and all of a sudden, your head is spinning as a consequence of all the solicited and unsolicited advice you are getting. For your emotional well-being, you buy books by very successful entrepreneurs, sports coaches, and politicians who claim that getting fired was the best thing that ever had happened to them. You read their inspiring stories, for example in Harvey Mackay's *We Got Fired!...And It's the Best Thing That Ever Happened to Us*. There is hope for you.

Then you start your job search without thinking much about it. As somebody who was happy in Corporate America before lay-off, you will not want to change your industry or type of company you have been working for. If you were not happy, you might start evaluating alternatives, like considering working for a non-profit organization, becoming a consultant, or joining a start-up or smaller company.

Should you be lucky and have access to an outplacement firm, they will get you started on a rigid timeline of finding your next job. The main benefit is the discipline their program gives you to help you drive your search process. Their tool set includes lots of information and resources, milestones-driven job search processes, seminars, online classes, and a personal advisor. They even offer networking groups with people in the same boat like you. Once the three or six month period that your company is paying is over, you hopefully have found a new fulfilling job. If you can get outplacement, use it. The process works.

THE "JOB SEEKER INDUSTRIAL COMPLEX"

A friend of mind coined the term "Marital Industrial Complex" to make a bit of fun of the business of getting married. From the ring (which must be of a certain size and value) to the flowers (which triple in price if the florist knows they are for a wedding), from the invitation cards to the right restaurant, from magazines covering weddings to personal wedding consultants, getting married is a business. It has become a "Marital Industrial Complex," indeed. Your wedding might be expensive, but you know that this important day of your life will be in good hands.

The job market industry is pretty similar. Just writing your CV and cover letter and sending both to a company of your choice—is that the way to do it? This would be way too simple. There is the full "Job Seeker Industrial Complex" available and begging to help you. Like in the "Marital Industrial Complex," the list of industry participants is broad: coaches for individuals, job boards for free, job boards to pay for as job seeker, business magazines, outplacement firms, career and self-help books, networking groups, pink slip parties, résumé writing services, search firms, seminars, etc...there is almost nothing that is not covered.

All have one common interest in mind: that you spend your time and money using their services with the promise of finding your next job. Both getting married and finding a job are similar in that the goal is to get to a long-term, enjoyable, and stable situation. In turn, people are prepared to make it right and invest a lot in getting there, both in terms of money and time.

As with any industry, there are some standards and rules involved when it comes to job search. These standards and rules make transactions and communication easier. That's why we have certain formats and recommendations about what to put on a résumé, how to write a cover letter, how much time to wait before calling a prospective company after submitting an application, and many more unwritten and written rules. They are very good for everybody involved. They make things easier, transparent, and help the job seeker avoid committing blunders.

THE PRESSURE POINTS CLOSE TO HOME: MONEY, FAMILY, AND FRIENDS

Parents, family, and friends can often be serious pressure points. They might be even more demanding than the "Job Seeker Industrial Complex." They all know you personally and will play with your emotions, consciously and unconsciously. Usually, everybody just wants the best for you. They keep calling to check how you are progressing. They *all* call. Or, alternatively, they don't ask you directly for a progress report for fear of getting the bad news that no job offer has been extended to you yet.

Sometimes, though, it is pure selfishness on your family's or friends' part. Friends fear that you might not have the money anymore to join them in expensive dinners without a job. Parents might be concerned that you will reduce the number of visits to them. Ex-colleagues want to see where you land a job to get a perspective on the job market and what they are worth. Neighbors jealous of your BMW just might ask to get a kick out of the fact that you still have not found a job yet. Spouses can worry about what the future holds, and children can feel embarrassed to tell the other kids at school that mom or dad became unemployed. These reactions are understandable, but you need to keep in mind that a person's emotions, no matter how much you love him or her, still belong to that person, not to you. I am not advocating that you should be insensitive, only that you not allow these kinds of concerns to throw you into panic mode.

There is another big concern you no doubt have—money. Unless you are independently wealthy, you need to work to make a living, feed your family, and pay the mortgage. Job loss is very unsettling. Even with severance payments, you know that the money won't last forever. Dreams of ending up as a greeter in Wal-Mart haunt you at night. You check your 401K, IRA, and other retirement and savings accounts frequently just to ensure that there is still something left.

All in all, unless you have a very strong will, the likelihood is high that you will just get on with the job search without much thinking and without much delay.

It is the right thing to do...or is it?

THE LIMITS OF CONVENTIONAL ADVICE TO JOB SEEKERS

Following common wisdom is usually a safe way to go about things. Nevertheless, there are few issues with just blindly following the associated rules and expectations. Both personal as well as surrounding economic circumstances might indicate that there might be a "better way," a "different approach" that fits your situation better.

If you view the "Job Seeker Industrial Complex" as such, you will not be surprised that it wants you to keep efficiently moving along from job loss through its industrial belt of job search to the final product of a having found a new job. For example, outplacement firms track and market their placement ratio. If you don't find a job before your company paid program ends, it is bad for their statistics and marketing claims. While the focus on efficiency can be very beneficial to the job seeker, you still should recognize that their incentives and yours are not necessarily 100% aligned.

Even worse, almost everybody around you will put the pressure of job search on you by instilling fear—"you are losing valuable time to look for a job," "you must be faster than other job seekers," and "how will you explain a three month hiking trip to a future employer?"—You get the idea.

The moment you show signs of breaking the rules, you are on your own. Following standards and common rules has a big advantage; it offers a mental safety net. You are mainstream, you don't need to explain yourself, and you don't have to think for yourself, which can be quite convenient. If things don't work out, you are not any different from the masses. Misery loves company. You become like a portfolio manager of a mutual fund that invests in stocks; he rarely buys securities different from what everybody else in similar funds is buying. Thus nobody can blame him for any bad performance of the fund, since the performance of all other funds will be similar.

Let's look at the questions that come to mind when conventional advice might fall short or not give the full answer:

- *State of the overall economy:* Is the advice of the "Job Seeker Industrial Complex" made for good economic times only, because it implicitly assumes that you will be finding a job in reasonable time? What if the doors are shut across the industry you are in? What to do in a deep recession with 10% or even 15% unemployment?

- *State of the industry you are in:* Looking at an industry going downhill like the automotive industry, how much good would it do to you as an ex-VP of Marketing in Detroit to start immediately looking? Where? At which company? Will jobs ever come back, even if the industry improves again one day? Should you move instead to Alabama for better opportunities?

- *Personal economic situation:* Does it make a difference if you are 50 years old vs. 30; whether you have severance vs. no severance; have no money in the bank vs. a great savings account? Doesn't more money give you more freedom and time? Or does it make you lazy and too relaxed to look for a new job?

- *Personal family situation:* Does it make a difference whether you are single or have a wife or husband? Can't you take more risks as a single person than a dad with a wife and two kids? Or would a family provide you with more emotional stability and potentially the safety of a second salary such that you can take on more risks than any single person ever could? Do you have a mortgage and high fixed costs and living expenses? Can they be reduced and by how much?

Individual needs: Isn't the common wisdom assuming that you want to continue the path you are on or know exactly what you want to do in case you want change? What if you are unsure what to do next? What is your level of "brain damage" from an intense career? How much time is "allowed" for thinking before you have to act? Four weeks? Four months?

Value of additional education: What about investing in some education and raising the odds of finding a better job later? How much would education help you find a job? How much time would it "buy" you in the job market?

Breaking the rules: Is it really true that you will not find a job unless you start looking immediately? Under what circumstances can it be that some successful people violated the mantra of immediate job search by taking one or even three years off, now having a better career than ever? Was it pure luck? Do the "rules" have exceptions?

The individual in "you": Is there no room for special situations in our country of opportunities, some flexibility for unconventional ideas? Are prospective employers all wired the same way? Do they all have a negative view of job seekers returning after a multi-month sabbatical? If you take a

41

year off during a recession, will you be considered a "genius" for timing or a "slacker"?

- *Trade-off of accepting a job just to be employed:* In good times, it is easy to find a new job at the same or higher salary. What happens in recessions with falling wages when too many applicants allow companies to reduce wages? If you take a 20% cut at the first job offered, will you ever get back to your former salary level? Couldn't there be a better strategy…just to wait and re-enter the labor market once conditions have improved?

- *What's the rush anyhow?* Given that total working years might total between 30 and 40, why the rush? Thirty to forty years of work equals 360 – 480 months. Can it really be that bad to take three-to-twelve months off and enjoy life, think and adjust your priorities? Shouldn't working 98–99% of your working lifetime be plenty? Shouldn't that be enough to pay for ongoing living expenses and savings for retirement?

All these questions might lead you to the conclusion that maybe, just maybe, applying for the next job right away might not be the best course of action.

WHAT IT MEANS TO START LOOKING FOR A NEW JOB

Looking for a job can be done either half-heartedly, or full time. Usually, you have to give it your all and be committed to have success. Looking seriously for a job is a job in itself, as any head-hunting company will tell you.

If you were let go on December 31, are you ready to jump right into the fray January 2? Didn't you just come out of a grueling time before and during the period when you lost your job? Haven't you just finished ten years working for the same company and never took more than two weeks vacation at a time? Aren't there many other things to do that you could do first before going at high speed into job search?

Listen to your own intuition. I strongly believe you have to be mentally ready to get back into the job market and not be panicky. "Mentally ready" means being at ease with the job opportunities you are pursuing and the location you are focusing on. It also means having the energy to conduct the search and being willing to start the new job immediately in case you might find new employment faster than expected. You should also be relaxed and not come across as desperate since any prospective company may easily sense panicky eagerness and turn you down.

I doubt that many who lose their job are in any productive stage of mental readiness immediately after they are let go. No matter how tough people are and what they say or what their economic situation is, job loss is usually a very emotional and energy draining affair. I think that the movie *Up in the Air* with George Clooney depicted quite well the emotional side of people who are let go. It's a grieving process, just like any other major loss in life. And if you don't give yourself time to grieve and recoup, you can carry unresolved anxieties into your new job. Instead of starting afresh, you'll be carrying old baggage.

When I lost my job, I was not mentally ready to go straight into full-time search. There were too many issues waiting to be

43

addressed. I postponed the outplacement services that were offered to me as far as I could to the time when I would be ready.

Take a closer look at the following chapters. See the opportunities that could come with the 15 alternatives to immediate job search. Don't apply for a job yet...read on first!

A NEW PERSPECTIVE —THE GIFT OF JOB LOSS

This book is called *The Gift of Job Loss* for a reason. I strongly believe that once you lose your job in Corporate America, no matter your level of hierarchy, it might be very unwise to go straight into full-time job search mode. You are handed a gift that you can choose to accept or reject. I hope that reading this book will encourage you to accept the gift when it presents itself to you.

There are a few exceptions to my advice of accepting the gift of job loss. Let me address them right upfront.

Some of you might be in exceptionally bad circumstances like unusual economic hardship (e.g., facing bankruptcy), a crippling health situation, sick parents to take care of, kids going off to university and stressing your finances, or if you're going through a divorce and are faced with the prospect of becoming a single parent, and other dire situations that make you truly desperate to find any job just to survive. By "any," I mean any job available to you, no matter whether it's desirable or not. If you are in such a situation, you have bigger things to worry about than many of the topics covered in this book. From the bottom of my heart I wish you luck and that your circumstances will improve fast.

Otherwise, people have a tendency to cite "lack of money" or "family" as a convenient excuse for not even considering things that might be in their own best interest. More specifically, having a mortgage, spouse with children, and getting laid off with six months of good severance pay does not qualify you for claiming "exceptional bad circumstances" and not giving my ideas a serious consideration! You might still decide to go right into job search, but then you do it based on self-awareness, not because of convention, reflex, or fear.

Part III and the *Appendix* will offer plenty of ideas and practical advice on how to deal with issues like money, family, and fear.

INTRODUCTION TO THE 15 ACTIVITIES OF THE GIFT OF JOB LOSS

What are you going to do with all the free time on your hands? What *should* you do? Fifteen possible activities come to mind. Remember, the day you are out of a job, you have the full day for you...the 8–10 hours you used to work, the time you commuted, and the time you dressed up.

It is all yours now! Take a look at the overview of all the activities listed. You will see two categories—7 no-regret activities that I believe you should pursue under any circumstances, and 8 optional activities. This is my subjective classification, of course. I strongly believe that the benefits of the 7 no-regret activities are truly outstanding and this group of activities be considered "must-dos" for everybody.

We will explore the individual activities one by one.

OVERVIEW

THE 15 ACTIVITIES OF THE GIFT OF JOB LOSS

THE 7 NO-REGRET ACTIVITIES:

1. Do nothing and enjoy your leisure activities.

2. Take a fun trip to a sunny spot and have passionate sex.

3. Stay healthy and improve your health.

4. Bring your life up to date and simplify it for the future.

5. Get your financial house in order.

6. Take at least one "once-in-a-lifetime" dream vacation.

7. Spend real quality time with a spouse, family member, or close friend.

THE 8 OPTIONAL ACTIVITIES:

8. Go back to school and get a degree or certification.

9. Learn a new language or something else that might be helpful in your main profession, secondary job, or in your daily life.

10. Do charity work.

11. Check out a different city or country to potentially work and live.

12. Find a mate, re-invest in your existing relationship...or use the time to get away from one that's not working.

13. Search for your true "calling" and decide on your future work-life balance.

14. Explore investment opportunities.

15. Explore career alternatives to Corporate America.

1 ▪ Do nothing and enjoy your leisure activities

If you are like most people, you like to do nothing for a while after something bad happens.

You might enjoy your morning coffee at 10 a.m. You could walk around in your neighborhood at 11 a.m. before watching some mindless TV shows for a good laugh at lunch time. In the afternoon you could catch up on reading the crime novel that has been languishing on your porch. Then you might drive the kids to soccer instead of your spouse. At night, you could enjoy the various leisure and sports activities you always liked.

The "do nothing" approach is good and very helpful for a few days and even a few weeks. You relax and get used to your new status as somebody "between jobs" or "starting out in a new direction." In fact, relaxing for a while might be the best method to calm down and let go of the old company ("those bastards—how dare they get rid of me, their best employee in the whole department!")

At this point, take it easy, and don't stress out over the future. Do not voluntarily make contact with your old co-workers from your office, unless they are close friends of yours. You must realize that the old company is now history. Every contact you make, every minute spent commiserating with those who were let go or are still employed there is just extending your agony.

The best thing you can do is to "declare victory." You achieve this by saying to yourself that you had a good time at your former employer; you met great people, had a good run, earned fair money, learned a few new tricks...and now you are ready for better things.

Declaring victory should help you focus on the good things you had in your old job. You might also think about the few bad

47

days there, since everything comes as a package. Every coin has two sides. Sit on your couch, close your eyes, enjoy your coffee or a glass of wine, and review the last months or years at your former employer. Think about the laughs you had, the times of crisis when you made things happen with your co-workers, the stupid boss you fooled. Be content that you had good employment so far and have a roof and shelter including a full fridge. Realize that you are part of the "lucky sperm club" by living in a democratic and peaceful country. Yes, count your blessings.

Ultimately, the "do nothing" period should not last too long, because it could sap your energy level and potentially depress you. Don't forget, there are so many other great things you can do with your life...remember, there are fourteen more activities to pick from apart from job hunting.

MY STORY

My "do nothing" period lasted for a few weeks, although before I left the company. Since New York State has mandatory notification laws in place, I had a 60-day window to prepare for the end of employment. I spent quite a few days on the couch with a cup of coffee, walked around my neighborhood, watched CNBC in the morning, and played the piano in the afternoon. I also got quite a bit of reading done.

2 ■ **Take a fun trip to a sunny spot and have passionate sex**

No matter what you decide to do—going quickly into a job search or taking a longer break, you need a fun trip first. The best spot is in the sun, at the beach, with good food and drinks, and passionate sex.

You need a break no matter what. A little escape is exactly what the doctor would order. One or two weeks to let off steam, get a tan, dance under the stars, sample exotic food, and realize that life is good, is the best bridge into the new phase of your life.

You might live in the northern part of the US where fall and winter can be long, dark, and snowy. Since many lay-offs seem to occur towards the end of the year, you should escape the darkness around you and have some mindless fun. Whether you pick Florida, the Bahamas, a last-minute cruise, or a resort in Mexico, it does not matter.

Getting away helps you relax and also put the past behind you. It clears your mind. When is the best time to go? I would say after you have "done nothing" (Activity #1) for a bit, at the beginning of your new status as unemployed. If you don't do it early, you might never do it and you will have a harder time disengaging in order to truly take on your new life.

The reasons that you should have passionate sex are as follows. Sex is one of the best mechanisms to relax—so say doctors. People who are too tired to have sex are those needing it the most. Studies show that when people are stressed at work, they don't even want to have sex anymore. A recent survey showed that 15% of married couples have not had sex during the last six months. I remember several articles about sexless marriages and couples in New York. People don't seem to have time for sex anymore. In fact, a casual, non-scientific survey among my friends and couples in New York revealed that none of them were making love on Friday nights. The exhaustion from the week was too big (luckily, many of them caught up over the weekends). Whether you belong to the stressed-out category or are lucky to be making passionate love several times a week, take your spouse, fiancé, girlfriend or boyfriend for a getaway, rekindle your fire, and enjoy! You both will feel much better upon return.

If you are single, well, I am sure you are aware of your options, from singles vacation clubs to more adventurous undertakings. Likewise, if you get no pleasure out of sex or it is just not your "thing," no problem. I encourage you to pick something else that delivers you utmost fun, out of the world relaxation, and full satisfaction—whatever gets your endorphin levels up, whatever puts you in a good mood and makes you laugh and a happy camper, just do it.

MY STORY

For me, the perfect getaway was Cartagena in Colombia. It was winter in New York, and sun and fun was necessary to lift my spirits. Our hotel offered nice pools, great views over the ocean, and a delicious breakfast buffet.

Cartagena surpassed all expectations. The city has nice museums in old buildings, be it the Museum of Modern Art or the Museum of the Spanish Inquisition. The atmosphere is serene and charming. You just like to be there at any time of the day or night. Cartagena is made for romantic evenings in fantastic restaurants, with local music on the streets, and lots of history to discover. By chance, we found our preferred restaurant that turned out to be the favorite hang-out of politicians including the President whenever he is in town. The seven-head strong band of seniors played Cuban inspired songs, and the seafood was delicious. It tasted like a cross between Caribbean and Argentine food. There was no better way to celebrate Valentine's Day.

Needless to say, I came back rested, relaxed, and fully satisfied…ready to continue the path of the gift of job loss.

3 ▨ Stay healthy and improve your health

Going to the gym, going on a bike ride, playing basketball with your buddies, sweating at yoga or strength training and cardio— whatever you do, it is well known that some type of physical activity is good for you. Thirty minutes on a treadmill will lower your risk of heart attack and diabetes. Other exercises will support a strong back. Pick up any magazine to learn about what is the latest and greatest exercise you can do. Enjoying sports also lifts your spirits and usually boosts your self-esteem.

No matter what activity you select, the key is that you do it. And here is where your free time comes in. You can now make a renewed effort to get into better shape. No matter your fitness level, there is no more excuse that you don't have time. It gets even better. You can take advantage of empty gyms during daytime (when other people work) and increase your regimen. You might even negotiate a better deal with the personal trainer to work with her or him during off-peak hours. If you are seriously overweight, the time might have come to enter a medically supervised program and change your dietary habits as well.

In other words, you are given the option to improve your health and increase your life span. Let me repeat that: Thanks to your lay-off, you are given the option to improve your health and increase the length of your life.

You might have some medical issues. You might have postponed taking care of them because you did not want to be absent from work. Maybe there is a benign tumor to be taken out. Or you need knee surgery that will cause you some restrictions in your movement and necessitate physical therapy for a while. Do it now! Now is the right time.

There is yet another benefit to getting in the habit of physical exercise. It is much easier to stay on course once you are used to it. Once you acquire the discipline, it is easier to keep up your exercise routine when you are going back to work.

MY STORY

I used my free time to lose a few pounds until I reached my ideal weight. I increased my frequency of going to the gym, hired a personal trainer, and tried a few new machines. More serious bicycling was also on the agenda. There were also the hikes in the mountains during my travel, but this was more the icing on the cake, not a daily routine. All in all small things, sure, but somehow I never had the time to deal with them while being employed. I kept my new routines alive after my time off.

4 ▪ Bring your life up to date and simplify it for the future

How many years have you been living in your place—a decade or more? How does your garage look, full of things you once thought you might need in the future? Have you already digitized your slides and pictures from the 80s and 90s to ensure they will live on for generations to come? What about your closet? The suits and t-shirts barely fit in the space, though it is already the third closet space you filled up. Oops, your shoes just fell off the rack—25 pairs were probably too many to stack there. And then there is your home office. You see bundles of old newspapers and National Geographics going back decades. Your place where you stuck gaudy old jewelry from long dead relatives doesn't look too good either. You always wanted to sell parts of them, in particular with the gold price so high these days. And didn't you want to call a local charity to pick up your old cranky piano that nobody is playing anymore? Yes, and if they could pick up the clunky TV as well, wouldn't that be great? And here is the latest Fortune magazine. Let's put it away on the table with the other dozen unread...Shall I go on?

Once we work, we rarely have time to significantly simplify our lives. Sometimes we do a good spring cleaning in our home, but most of us carry a long list of things we never get around to doing. Things that clutter our lives sometimes are even costly, like the subscriptions we picked up years ago. Our homes are full of toys from kids that are grown up, old bikes that do not function anymore, and paper is everywhere.

Here is your chance. Once you are done "doing nothing," have had your fun trip, and are in the midst of getting healthier, you can focus your attention on home improvement. You still get up at 10 a.m., if you are inclined to do so, but now you spend two hours or more a day emptying out stuff you have not touched in a year, call up charities, sell used items on *Craigslist*, and make your home tidy and clean. Go through your files and shred old bills and toss out everything you don't need anymore. Optimize your family pictures and re-arrange any furniture. Recycle old magazines and make room for new clothes. Clean up your email accounts. Fix things that are broken.

I know you may hate doing this, but this is your chance to bring your life up to date and make room for something "new." The advantages will be multifold. First, cleaning out clutter is therapeutic and it is free. Once you get going, you see how your home becomes nicer, less cluttered, and you feel a burden taken off your shoulders. The more you give away, the more you get organized, the more subscriptions and digital cable programs you cancel, the better you feel. You will also like the feeling of doing something good and picking up a tax receipt for your donations when giving to charity.

There might be even bigger items that you postponed dealing with. You still might be living in a big house, but now you are an "empty nester." Now you have the time to think about alternatives, like moving into a condo or smaller home. Or upgrading or down-sizing your car. It is so much more pleasant talking to a car sales-man on a Tuesday morning than on a crowded Saturday.

MY STORY

I probably got rid of 30% of my belongings—recycling of papers, furniture for charity, and selling a few goods. I loved it. Less was more. And despite this cut, I still felt I had not cut enough when I later moved from New York to Austin.

5 ■ Get your financial house in order

If your finances appear to be fine, nevertheless take a close look at your financial situation and ensure you are aligned with what you want to accomplish and with your new context of being without a job. There are three powerful reasons why the time has come to take stock of your financial life.

First, you now have the time to look at all your assets (home, 401K, IRAs, savings accounts, rental properties, etc.) and debt (mortgage, student loans, credit card debt, installment loans) and see where you are at. Taking stock every few years (some advisors recommend once a year) is important for you to have transparency in your financial health.

Second, the fact that you are now unemployed most likely means that you should cut some discretionary spending, reduce your fixed costs, and probably consider conservative and income producing securities (e.g., CDs, bonds) that offer some stability.

Third, looking ahead the next 6–18 months, you should consider some scenarios and see what they mean for your income and spending and what you can afford or not afford. This is one area where I do recommend that you get professional help, if you are not financially proficient yourself. You can find professional fee-based-only advisors that are not conflicted by commissions on *www.napfa.org*.

The main point is that you should pull out your bank statements, IRA/401K and brokerage statements, your severance package material, your cell phone bill, your car expenses, your mortgage payments, and take stock of everything. The exercise might surprise you. You might detect that you are richer than you thought you would be. Or you might be shocked to learn how many thousands of dollars per year you spend on cell phone, home phone, Internet, and cable TV. Buy a good book on personal finances, a calculator, get your binders...and start the exercise. Thanks to having time now, there is nobody stopping you from spending a few days getting a good grip on your finances and for you to start making adjustments immediately.

Your financial advisor might help you consolidate retirement accounts and come up with the right financial plan for your specific situation. You might use your severance money to pay down debt (see *Appendix B: A Primer on Severance Policies*). You might cancel expensive TV channels, superfluous magazines, and data plans for your telecommunication devices. In any event, I would be surprised if you were not able to make some meaningful changes that should set you up better for the months and years ahead.

You also should take a hard look at any real estate you own. First, the one you live in. Does it fit your future needs? Could you get something better and cheaper? Do you have a smaller second home or vacation home that might be just the right thing for the next stage of your life? Maybe it is time to sell your principal home, take the money, and downsize. Or maybe you will need to sell your vacation home if you don't plan on going there a lot.

If money is of no concern to you, you might then decide to get an even bigger home if you really need it. Alternatively, if you come to the conclusion that no change is needed, that's fine, but at least you did your homework and based your assessment on the relevant facts.

Don't forget to analyze your tax situation. State taxes vary widely within the country. And the tax code is not stable over time. For example, in 2010 there were new rules on who can convert from a tax-deferred IRA to a tax-free retirement account (Roth). Since you would have to pay ordinary income taxes on the conversion amount, you saved more than 10% or more in taxes when doing this in Florida or Texas rather than in New Jersey. While you cannot escape the state taxman on severance payments (they are taxed where earned, no matter where you live by the time of payment), there are many items up for optimization. Get a tax professional to help you. The time of unemployment might offer some hidden gems on the tax side for you to dig out.

MY STORY

I adjusted my portfolio by moving to more income producing securities and realized some tax losses. Moreover, I left expensive New York City and moved to Austin. The savings from my rent of my nice one-bedroom apartment in New York alone would pay for most of my activities during my time off. The math was amazing. Austin would become the perfect "base camp" for time off. A mortgage for double the space would cost half the rent of a one-bedroom in Manhattan. I reasoned that even if I had to move right back to the Big Apple in case a job came up, the relatively low cost of a move compared to the high housing costs in New York made this a great deal. As a bonus, any income from savings and dividends would be taxed only at the federal level since Texas has no income tax.

6 ▪ Take at least one "once-in-a-lifetime" dream vacation

The gift of job loss is amazing. No need to explain to your boss why you would like a four-week vacation that would exceed your annual allowance. No need to bargain for a "leave of absence" or sabbatical. You are free and can do so at any time and length you like. Whether you want to follow Formula One around the world, cross the US by bike, cross the Andes by horse, join a cruise to Antarctica, or walk the Appalachian Trail, it's all up to you. Your time has come and it might not come again in the foreseeable future. In *Part II* you have to think very hard about how you spend your lifetime and what the trade-off of money and time means for you. Taking a dream vacation after lay-off is one of many decisions you should contemplate.

Many things don't come back in life. You might like to visit the Pyramids in Egypt—go for it, it is safe now, but a few years ago terrorists caused a massacre among tourists near a famous temple. You might like to hike Kilimanjaro in Africa—better do it now, as long as your health is still strong enough to weather the high altitude. You might like to visit Machu Picchu—do it now before the government triples the admission numbers and you might not recognize this world heritage site anymore. You might like to drive around in beautiful New Zealand, home of many movies like *The Lord of the Rings*—do it now as long as you can still stomach the 24-hour flights and have the capacity to drive a car or mobile home in a different country. You might like to take your spouse on a "halfway around the world" cruise for 90 days—do it now as long as your dollars are still worth something and not eaten by inflation.

The point is that you don't know the future. Your risk of not doing your dream travel now is that you might never be able to do it due to factors outside your control. There is no right or wrong here in terms of how long you want to travel, how often, or where. Or even just stay close to home and explore your own county or state, if that's your dream. The key is that you should create or look at your personal "bucket list," analyze the dreams you might have forgotten about, and just pursue them.

MY STORY

I have a bias for travel. For me, it's the best part of the gift of job loss. No time restrictions, no Blackberry to check, plenty of time to see many destinations on my list. I traveled to twelve countries in a series of short and multi-week trips. Countries visited included Egypt, Iceland, Jordan, Peru, Poland, and Uruguay, just to name a few. Clearly, for me, the "once-in-a-lifetime dream vacation" activity category was one of my favorites. If you want to see some mouthwatering pictures to make you wish you could travel to these places immediately, check out www.thegiftofjobloss.com.

7 ▪ Spend real quality time with a spouse, family member, or close friend

Parents, kids, spouses, nieces and nephews, godfathers and god-mothers, aunts and uncles, grandmas and grandpas, grandsons and granddaughters, cousins in foreign countries—the list of family members can be staggering. Some of them you see all the time and are in close contact with, some you don't talk to often, some might live far away, for many you might not even care.

Now the time has come to spend more time with your family. There could be a long postponed trip to take your dad to France or your family on a road trip to Calgary. There could be the trip with Mom back to India to meet the whole big family in Kerala, the family you never saw since you were born here

59

in the US. Or maybe it is time to build rapport with a far-away cousin with whom you had a family issue years ago. Or just take your granddaughter for a full five days to Disney World and Epcot Center in Florida, the five days you never wanted to invest of your ten days you had during the years when you were employed.

Whether your motive is past promises that are to be fulfilled like a certain vacation with your parents, the avoidance of future regret if you did not make a visit to a sick relative, or the pure joy of spending more time with someone special, now is the right time to do it. Close to home, what about just enjoying playing "stay-at-home dad" for a while and see little Johnny grow up for a few weeks or months? As a formerly working mom, wouldn't it be nice not to worry about the nanny or daycare (and the expenses associated with childcare), but spend the full day with your sweet little daughter?

Only you know your family situation. Given that time makes kids grow up fast, makes family members we love get old, sick, and ultimately die, having time on hand is invaluable.

The topic of work-life balance is not new and there are many great books on how to deal with it. Unfortunately, they only offer mostly little fixes. Most humans are not superhuman enough to be as ruthlessly efficient as prescribed in these books! The main driver of your daily professional time spent—both number of hours and distribution during the day and night—is driven by your job choice.

When you pick a profession, you know or will quickly learn the rules. When and how do your colleagues work? Is work performance and compensation tied to real performance or to just showing up? Are people rewarded for sending out emails on Sunday, for signaling (but in reality just pretending) that they do work 24/7? Don't believe me? I once had a boss who knew how to play the corporate game. She was proud to tell everybody at her team's holiday party in front of her husband that every Sunday over brunch she was swapping emails with another colleague, which was indeed true. Of course, this was all show, no substance or necessity. But if this is the type of company you pick, you know that instead of playing with your kids on Sunday morning, you will be on your cell phone, or even worse, in your office.

You cannot change these rules. It is "love it or leave it." Kids vs. money, family time vs. big bonus. These can be stark choices, though sometimes only in your head, a self-inflicted hardship. Only you can decide.

A similar and maybe even more brutal trade-off: How much time do you spend with your parents as they grow old? Well, let's say you and your spouse live in Chicago, but your only surviving parent, your mother, has a house in San Diego. How often do you see her? How often can she come to visit until her deteriorating state of health intervenes? Didn't you promise her five years ago to travel with her to the countryside of Ireland where her family roots are? You finally planned the trip for Memorial Day weekend of last year, but then your boss asked you for this special project and you relented. No worries, Mom, we can do Ireland in September. Too bad, you got a promotion in July and then needed to travel to Asia to introduce yourself as the new Head of Finance for Asia to the management teams of your enlarged area of responsibility. Mom understood. In order to ensure that you really would take Mom the Memorial Day of *this* year, you bought the tickets immediately. In November, though, you got the dreadful phone call. Your mom suddenly had just passed away. Every year of your life on the day of her passing's anniversary you will remember your broken promise of the trip to Ireland that was always second priority.

Yes, indeed, some things don't come back. Being laid-off from work is one of the great opportunities to catch up on promises to family members. That is why it is a no-regret activity in my book.

MY STORY

In my case, I took my mom to the place where she was born but had never returned to after she and her parents had to flee at the end of WWII. She was 74 years old and it was now 64 years after she had to leave her hometown as a nine-year-old while the bombs fell and the winter killed tens of thousands of refugees. The only things left from these days were some old maps and some pictures from the house she had lived in, the school, church, and kindergarten. For years she had wanted to go back and see whether she would recognize the city that was now supposed to be beautifully reconstructed. What a great moment we had when we found the house where she was born, the school, and the church—about two generations later. It was amazing and very emotional.

After having looked at the 7 no-regret activities, let's now turn to the 8 optional activities among which you should pick those most applicable to you.

8 ▩ Go back to school and get a degree or certification

Education and certifications are often still the path to riches, prestige, and advancement. This signals to employers a certain standard and skill set you bring with you. No matter how old you are or what degree you already have under your belt, there is probably something you can do.

If you are in your thirties or forties or even fifties when losing your job, would it make sense to go back to school? On the surface, a wide choice seems available. There are university programs (college, post-graduate), vocational programs, and many for-profit educational programs.

This book cannot give you an overview of everything out there nor really help you with such a decision. Whatever certification or degree you might aspire to, it means spending some time and money.

At least, I can share with you my general thoughts. Here are just a few guidelines that come to mind:

First, distinguish whether you want to start something new (let's say you change fields from IT project manager to health care service provider) or do something in your area of expertise. Take a look at your passion and see what professions are up and coming or even expected to be big in a few years. For example, *The Wall Street Journal* (May 16, 2010) reported promising occupations of the future in its article "What will be the hot jobs of 2018?" which is based on the Labor Department's *Occupational Outlook Handbook.*

If you start something new, the decision to go to school is part of a broader decision to retool your life and the investment in the option to go for it. It usually means you have a new long-term horizon for something new that warrants your time and money. You might also have longer lead times to get into a program, since your lay-off might not correspond with the application cycle of the school you desire.

If you go for something in your own field, I would choose those designations that really help you to get to the next level. For example, if you are a middle manager with cost-cutting experience, getting a Six-Sigma, LEAN, or Program Manager Certification might be a good choice. If you are an accountant, the time might be ripe to invest in a corresponding designation as an option for your next move up.

Education providers are offering all kinds of degrees. Make sure that whatever you pursue is somehow accredited, teaches you something new, and has a history of helping people advance in their careers. Be very careful going into uncharted waters by signing up for degrees that are new on the market. Nobody might know them, and they might be worthless.

Third, look for tax credits and other programs that might help you with the costs. Continued education in your field is usually tax deductible; entering a new field may not be.

MY STORY

In my case, going back to school was not on the agenda. I like being in my field and would not like to start something totally new that needs years of education. This does not mean that one day in the future I might not go back to school to study music history or Spanish literature, should I still be mentally fit in old age.

9 ▪ Learn a new language or something else that might be helpful in your main profession, secondary job, or in your daily life

I have to admit a certain bias here. Feeling like a global citizen and seeing how the world is coming closer together, the advantage of having language skills is becoming more valuable every day. Speaking foreign languages gives you more options in terms of jobs available to you, and more countries to work in.

Learning a language has other advantages as well. Given that the older we get, the more difficult it is to learn a language, this activity keeps our brain cells young. Studying grammar, translating and analyzing texts, watching foreign films, and conversing with people in your non-native language might even help prevent Alzheimer's.

There is also the fun factor. If you like French songs, wouldn't it be nice to understand what they were singing? If your kids learn Spanish in school, how much fun would it be to learn in parallel with them and figure out the homework together?

It is very time consuming to learn a language. CDs/DVDs and other programs for a little money invite you to learn a language "10 minutes a day," but like commercials for home trainers, there is a 99% chance that you will not reach the desired results. Only a teacher, ideally a native speaker, can give you the discipline to carry out your studies, correct your pronunciation, give and correct homework, and answer questions. No online tutorial or CD/DVD will get you there. Moreover, to really immerse yourself, you should spend time in a country of the language in question.

If you invest four weeks on the ground and take four hours a day—a standard program—you will be able to speak the language in a daily situation. If you invest three months of study, you can reach a good level of fluency. And how much hardship would it be for you to spend three months in Rome or another great city? Or enjoying the University of Salamanca in Spain, or placing you in the cosmopolitan city of Buenos Aires in Argentina? Your choice does not have to be black or white. You can start with some CDs/DVDs or join a group class in your home town to get a feel for things, then go to a specific language study program, and then pick a language school in a foreign country. Learning, making new friends, plus seeing all the tourist sites over the weekends can be an unforgettable experience.

Many programs are arranged by universities and are reasonably priced. The choice of where to study also influences your costs greatly. The widest choice offers Spanish—from one-on-one lessons for $3 per hour in Antigua, Guatemala, to $50 per hour in Spain, you can pick whatever fits your financial and touristy needs.

Maybe you have had some Spanish in school, or maybe even some French. Taking some time now to improve your skills to a reasonable level of fluency, maybe getting a certificate attesting to your skills, or taking classes for business language purposes might pay off later when re-applying for a new position. I am not aware of any activity that combines learning, fun, and tourism in such an attractive mix as learning or improving your language skills.

Some of you might say that you barely mastered English well and make spelling and grammar mistakes. If this is an issue, then you should consider using your free time to improve your English skills first before anything else. It is a bit harder to find programs teaching native speakers to become better in English, but there are some choices. From books teaching you grammar with exercises to vocational classes, writing classes, or even getting a private tutor—there are ways to improve your English. This investment will be worth it. You can also think about supplementing your mastery of the language by combining it with speaking skills; there are many groups out there (e.g., Toastmasters) that could help you.

In the movie *Up in the Air*, George Clooney, playing a consultant who helps companies dismiss employees, fires an older employee. He tries to cheer him up by pointing out that the latter had put cooking on his CV and that the time might have come to consider making this hobby a profession. What might seem cynical and an attempt to prevent the employee from going postal actually has something encouraging to it.

You could look at your hobbies and bring them up "to the next level" of proficiency. Be it a musical instrument, learning a trade, singing, or becoming a mechanic, the opportunities are virtually endless. You could go to cooking school, for a new career, a secondary job, or just to impress your spouse, and do more home cooking. If you are into photography, maybe join a workshop series hosted by a world famous photographer and earn some extra income after that. If yoga is your cup of tea, why not try becoming an instructor yourself? If you are a gifted writer, why not take it to the next level? Again, not necessarily for a full-blown career change, but for that little extra income, or that little extra satisfaction the new level of mastery will provide you in the future.

Since all these classes and courses take time and effort, you probably would never have had the chance to pursue them with success during your last job. That is why you did not learn these skills earlier. The moment you start a new position you will lack the time again. It is now when your job loss is handing you such an opportunity on a golden platter that you should not turn it down lightly.

MY STORY

For me, getting Spanish up to fluency and being able to prove it, was a personal goal of mine. Professionally, I had spent quite some time in Latin America off and on. It had always disturbed me that I had to conduct meetings in English. This had to change and mastery of the language would be great for any new job dealing with Spanish-speaking countries. Moreover, I am a big fan of tango and other music from Latin America. Gaining fluency would pay off every day in my home when listening to music. Since I only learn when I have deadlines, I picked a certain proficiency level I wanted to reach within a given time frame. I decided to sit for a five-hour exam administered by the Spanish government. My excitement was huge when I learned later that I had passed. It had been 15 years since my last exam. I felt like a little boy opening holiday gifts.

10 ▪ Do charity work

During the spring of 2009 in New York, many of the unemployed joined charities or got involved in their communities. This was not only good for the respective charities, but also for the folks doing it. Charity work is a very American thing to be proud of. Many of us either give money to our favorite causes, or donate time, or both.

Apart from the feeling of doing something meaningful and making a difference, joining a charity has some additional benefits for you. First, you are not bored and sitting alone at home. You are out with people on a joint mission. This alone might keep you from getting depressed or thinking too much about the future. There might even be opportunities for networking through charity work. You meet new people in your church organization, the animal shelter, the symphony, whatever organization you pick. If you choose a cause that is very important for you personally, let's say gay rights or a libertarian message, you can put your philosophy and conviction to great use. Finally, you might be able to put your charity work on your résumé when applying for your next job. It will seem like an extra bonus in your favor to potential employers. You help make the world a better place, make new contacts, feel good, and it might even raise your chances of finding the next job.

As a reader of this book, you probably work in the for-profit sector and want to stay there. For some of you, though, shifting to a non-profit could be a great way to start a new chapter in your life. If you are good at raising funds and marketing, maybe you can test out becoming a fundraiser. If you have a social work degree and never really liked Corporate America in the first place, now might be the time to shift careers (see Activity #15).

Charity work can also be done outside the US. There are many organizations that need your skill set. When I was in Guatemala, I met Americans and Canadians who helped build homes. Apart from enriching the lives of those who needed it most, they learned some Spanish on the way. You could do the same. Select an organization and location where charity can help you learn or improve a language as well. There is nothing wrong with combining doing charity work while at the same time doing something for you.

MY STORY

My time off led to something exciting. I am now sponsoring the English language education of a little girl in Guatemala, the daughter of a severely handicapped mother. Mastering English will hopefully allow the girl to leave poverty behind by working in tourism or in a company. The idea came up spontaneously during my weeks of taking Spanish lessons. I searched for education options and finally found a local language school that offers classes for kids. The school has to report progress and I promised to continue supporting the child until adulthood, assuming regular attendance. No intermediary organization is involved in my little charity. If I had not spent time abroad, this opportunity to help would never have come up. I sincerely hope that it will be successful.

11 ▪ Check out a different city or country to potentially work and live

Given your scarce vacation time, you probably didn't have enough time to check out a different location you might think to be a better place to live and work. You could be in Chicago and your sister is telling you all the great things about Boulder, Colorado. Or your kids are in Miami raving about the wonderful opportunities in real estate now. Or your city is in economic decline and you feel it might be time to move.

Cities and even countries, like industries, have their life cycles and offer different benefits and downsides. Here is a mistake you can make: you are so drawn to finding a job where you live that you disregard your surroundings. You can be in the wrong location.

The city you live in determines to a large degree your career and even mating options. There is nobody better than Richard Florida with his book *Who's Your City?* to illustrate this point. Florida makes a good case for the impact of cities on our lives. A city that might be right for us when young might not be the best later in life. A college town with cheap housing and many young folks is appealing when you are college age, but less so when retired. He distinguishes five life periods—recent college graduates, young professionals, family with children, empty-nesters, and retirees—and describes the typical needs in each. He then matches each life period with the top cities in the country for each category.

Selecting the right city is important along two timelines: first, the city should match your life stage and personality. Second, the trends of the city's economic development should be positive for your job and living prospects.

If for example you take a look at Austin, Texas today, you see private construction downtown, residential towers, office space, but also meaningful public works in infrastructure. In other words, it is a vibrant city, on the upswing, with low unemployment, an ever-increasing population, a city that the *Economist* magazine just recently featured as one that got things right. The time might be right for you to move to Austin!

Generally speaking you want to live in a city or region on the upswing. Beyond financial reasons, there are simple aesthetic reasons as well. A rich city plants trees and flowers, the streets are clean, the potholes few, and culture and art can thrive. Cities moving downhill like Detroit are closing parks, as the *Wall Street Journal* reported.

Now, let's expand our point of economic trends from your city to the country you live in. This might be a strange thought for you given the US has been the "number one" economy worldwide for the last 50 years. There have been a few recessions, some wars in far away lands, but no real setbacks. Living standards have never been higher, medical advancements occur daily, and the US is still the greatest country for years to come.

Or is it?

Well, when it comes to economic trends and the US, for the first time I can remember, quite a few analysts, economists, and political experts, have been voicing their doubts and asking whether this crisis is different and whether our economic situation is merely a cyclical downturn or something more structural...like a bigger version of Detroit, so to speak.

The optimists declare this pessimism as hogwash. The US is resourceful. It has always overcome difficulties in the past, be it wars or economic challenges, like Japan in the eighties. No country has the brainpower and the freedom to express and use it like us. Followers like India and China are light years away from getting even close economically or politically. No other country has the combination of centuries-old democracy and economic liberty like the United States; nobody offers such stability for investments and people.

You have to come to your own conclusion when choosing where to live. Sometimes the good times don't come back during your lifetime or it takes a decade for things to improve like the decade of long depression in the 1930s.

Should you lose your job during bad economic times or in a city caught in a downward spiral, this is your push to get a ticket to literally "ride out of town." You can use any severance and unemployment payment to explore something in a different location. There is an economic boom always somewhere. Being unemployed might give you a great incentive and the time to explore even options outside the US. Many countries like Canada, Chile, and even several countries in the European Union desperately need many of the skills US employees bring to the table and offer visas for those that have them.

If you are employed, you can apply for a job in a different city, but this is difficult. Many companies are reluctant to pay for travel costs just to interview you. Also, it takes time to fly to and from a location, potentially eating into your valuable vacation time. Fly twice and you will be down 2–4 days of your annual allocation. Even if everything works out and you get the job offer, moving to a different location is a serious matter.

How much better is the situation for you after you get laid off! You have no time restriction on checking out a new location. You might need two weeks or two months to get a good feel for a new potential place. You might even check out several places, one in the US, one abroad. You can customize time and effort to your needs. Being on the ground makes it also much easier to talk to local companies, headhunters, friends, and acquaintances through social networks. All of them can help you get a better understanding and act as a reality check to your imagination and expectations. It is your test ride. If you like what you see, your resolve to move is strengthened, and you know you are on the right track. By the same token, you might be surprised to figure out that Boulder is too young for you, or Miami too humid, and realize you better stay put where you are. Either way, you make a great decision based on facts. And these facts you were only able to gather thanks to the time you have had on hand.

MY STORY

I moved from New York City to Austin. Since my graduate studies, I had been making visits to friends there. These trips had kept me abreast of the fantastic transformation of the city. I did not need time to check it out to raise my knowledge about it, though mentally, I am viewing my move as a one or two-year trial instead of a 2–4 week trial that you might do. In the same vein, most of my travel went to Latin America, another option for me in the long run, be it for professional reasons or for retirement. Thus, in a way, I used my time off to check out both domestic and international locations.

12 ▪ Find a mate, re-invest in your existing relationship...or use the time to get away from one that's not working

If you are happily married or have otherwise found your significant other for the rest of your life, skip this section. You are done! Just use your time wisely to keep your relationship happy. If you have neglected your spouse during the last years, though, now use your time to do everything to make up for it and ensure your relationship stays on track. Invest the time available to be the caring and loving person you want to be; the moment you start working again, you will be back to the same old routine and trade-off between your professional and personal life. Your investment of time into your relationship may earn you brownie points with a pay-off over years to come.

If you are single, or thinking about "upgrading," read on!

We all know that being unemployed does not sell very well at cocktail parties. Nor is it a winner when trying to impress the other gender.

"Hi, I am John" "How do you do? I'm Stacey." "What do you do here in Chicago, John?" "Hmmmm, well, I am between jobs, you know, trying to find something new after they fired me...." "Nice to meet you, John, let me get a drink, see you later."

This wasn't very good, right?

Let's try this again:

"Hi, I am John" "How do you do? I'm Stacey. What do you do here in Chicago, John?" "I am taking six months to travel the world; I am just here for a few days to empty my mailbox and come to this party. I have just come back from India, where I visited the Taj Mahal, Mumbai, and the beautiful region of Kerala. And next Saturday I am off to Guatemala to do some charity work." "Wow, that is amazing. Are you independently wealthy or a student with too much time on his hands?"

"No, not at all, Stacey, I accepted severance in the current crisis and I am now using my free time to allow myself to realize some dreams that I always had. I admit, my savings of the last few years are helping, but travel is pretty cheap these days and no need to sleep in huts. Are you interested in seeing some amazing pictures from India?" "Absolutely, John, this is so interesting. I love Indian Bollywood movies, but I have never been to India. Here is my business card with my phone number. Please call me before you leave again. Please do, really."

This was much better. The story is better; so is the underlying message. The moment you do not view yourself as unemployed, as a panicky corporate slave waiting for the next ship to take you to your next owner, the mating game can be in your favor. Your story of amazing travel and independence will go a long way with your romantic prospects. You are not stressed; you radiate exuberance, financial stability, and maturity. You know what you want; you can handle this world. It was your decision to accept severance; it was almost planned.

Unless you are lucky and run into your future partner in the streets of your home town walking to the bakery (it happened to a good friend of mine), you have to go where the mating market is, right? You need to go out dancing, join a hiking club, show up at cultural events, mix and mingle at social events, enjoy your best friend's party, and so on. Unless you go out and search strategically in places where the chances of finding your perfect match are the highest, you are not spending your time wisely.

Now enter your past work life. You spent hours at work and maybe even some weekends. You were stressed. You optimized your career. You found great people online or wherever, but going out on dates was only possible Friday or Saturday night for you. During the week, you needed to travel, worked late or had to take care of other things. Too bad, though, that each and every year has only 52 weekends of which many are "occupied" by public holidays, family obligations, being in bed with a cold, weekends with good old friends, parents coming to town, doing some charity work, or moving apartments. Thus courtship had to be very efficient. You didn't have too much time. Dinner, movies, maybe a bike tour together, but then something came up that you did not like about her or him...and that was it. You are still single.

I just saw a two-page ad by the dating agency *It's just lunch*. Their clever proposal is to use your lunch time that you are spending anyhow (you need to eat, right?) to meet somebody for a date. As proof of their concept, their ad showed a nice graph. Singles were asked about their roadblocks to finding the right person. About 21% answered that they didn't have the time to find people they would be interested in dating. Over 60% considered it difficult to find the right places to meet their match.

The trade-off of a hard-charging career with long working hours and finding a mate is crystal clear to many but sometimes not to the career-minded singles themselves. Maybe New York is extreme and where you live things are different. The Big Apple is full of the most beautiful, accomplished people working for the most prestigious firms. Many successful women are in their late thirties or early forties, single, no kids....and now longing for a baby (same goes for many guys). Time went by quickly and the

77

focus was on career. Unfortunate and tragic if you think the following: you still might be able to earn millions in your fifties, sixties, seventies, and eighties, but the biological clock stops ticking eventually, no matter what Hollywood stars suggest. Some things, or times, don't come back.

Having plenty of time now is a big plus. Internet dating, going to social functions, trying to meet people at church, joining a local bicycle tour—it all takes time. Now you can go on your search several hours a day, seven days a week. Monday evening you learn Spanish in a group class, Tuesday you do Pilates, Wednesday you join a lunch at the local museum, and then off to an Internet date with somebody who is self-employed. Thursday you go out with a group of friends. Friday you meet another Internet date from a different site. During the week-end, you go all in. Saturday morning, you cruise a book store's "love and romance" area, then off to the coffee shop where your kind of gal or guy hangs out. After another lunch date from one of the Internet sites you join a local charity's activity. Then you rush home to change clothes because a gallery opening is waiting for you where you collect more phone numbers from attractive prospects for follow-up. Sunday morning, after church, you enjoy the social gathering where you happily chat up a few more people.

Think about it. Instead of doing the regular thing—job first, mate later—you turn it around. Mate first, job later. I am not saying that you *should* do it this way, but you *could*. You have the time now. If you are still looking for a mate, start spending your time strategically and invest in what is dearest to you.

The brother of a friend of mine did exactly that in the recession of 2002. As an ex-investment banker he had never found the time to focus on dating outside his demanding job. Freshly unemployed, he shifted his attention 100% and ultimately found what he was seeking.

If you are in an unhappy relationship, you might now have a chance to get out more easily. You can play the "I am poorer now" card and your partner might let you go with less emotional burden than otherwise. Also, a divorce might be financially easier and keep the financial demands of your soon to be ex-spouse in check.

If you live with somebody and want to move out, again, time works in your favor. It is much easier to pack, organize a move, and find something better than to be tossed out over the weekend and then have to show up to work on Monday morning.

Finally, if you are in a strained relationship, but need some "distance" to reflect upon the situation, you now have the chance to do so. Take a trip alone to contemplate your current state of relationship in order to decide what to do with it—break up or make up?

MY STORY

I arrived at the national departure area of Guatemala Airport at 5 am. Everything was still quiet and almost dark. TAG, Guatemala's airline, operates about two flights a day with a small 12-seater to Flores, the gateway to the world famous Mayan ruins of Tikal. After a while, people were showing up including the check-in staff. I noticed a woman who was looking intensively at her guide book. Clearly a tourist, I thought. All the others seemed local. We boarded and I slowly woke up as we ascended for our one-hour flight. The tourist woman was in front of me. I peered over her shoulder and I saw that she was reading a German guide book. I talked to her and it turned out that she was, not surprisingly, like me, on her way to Tikal. She was a German co-owner of an IT-company. Like me, she was spending a few weeks in the beautiful town of Antigua for Spanish language immersion, though taking lessons at a much higher level than me. She was already fluent! We started talking and finally decided to take the same guided tour. I had, stupidly enough, agreed at the travel agency to go for an English speaking tour, while she had booked the Spanish version. Bueno! I managed to join her tour. This was a very wise choice. We were the two only tourists and had a phenomenal local Spanish only speaking guide. He walked for six hours over ten miles with us on what was supposed to be only a four-hour program. He showed us wild animals, pointed out beautiful flowers, explained the myth and history of the place, explained Mayan art, and made us climb steep temples to have views over the jungle around us. We had the time of our lives. During these hours, we started to get to know each other. Later, I was able to convince her to extend her trip by one day and join me in Yaxhá, another, though less visited Mayan site made famous through Survivor Guatemala. She took the risk. At this point I did not know yet that we would become a couple soon!

13 ▪ Find your true "calling" and decide on your future work-life balance

Finding your true calling is much more than just a job decision. It involves your whole life—from where to live, how to live, what to do, how to set priorities, and yes, in what capacity you choose to work from this point onward.

If you feel that you have not yet found your true destiny, you might start with New Age books and get inspired by Paul Coelho's *The Alchemist*, then progress to various business book authors. The self-help section of every bookstore offers a great choice of both novels (intended to inspire you), and non-fiction books (intended to help you examine your needs). In my literature overview (*Appendix C*), I will give you a short reading list.

Contemplation is a funny thing. It can lead you to the best and the worst results. Since you have time on your hands, you have a unique opportunity to evaluate where you stand in life and what you want to get out of it. This fits right into the big question of how to maximize your life and lifetime, a key issue that we will address in *Part II*. You can take this journey alone, with your partner, a coach, or all of the above. Maybe you are now in your forties, have achieved a lot, but not all that you wanted, and realize it is now time to make some tough choices— career vs. more time spent with family, starting your own business before you get too old, moving to the place where your aging parents live. You might have postponed some decision making while being employed, either for lack of time or on purpose as an excuse, telling yourself that you don't have time to deal with certain issues. Now your time has come.

It is also a great time to think about the work-life balance that is usually driven by your profession. This is even more important if you are a woman in your late thirties and your dream of having children has not been fulfilled yet. You could change tracks and find a profession that is not too time-demanding.

There is no law that says that only jobs with long work hours can make you rich or happy. In short: pick something where you can work smart, not hard. Pick an industry or company where the profit goal is less pronounced than other values. Elect a profession that allows you to work part-time, work from home, or start your own business on your own terms. Consider moving to a (European) country with better working conditions including generous maternity leaves.

The biggest risk of contemplation and reading self-help books is that you might get confused fast and lose your footing. Let's assume that you really enjoyed working for a big corporation, notwithstanding your recent job loss. Now you see all these books on how to escape from Corporate America and how to become a consultant or start your own business. You start having self-doubts. Are you missing something? Is there anything you should be aware of? Are you the last man standing by feeling happy in a big corporation and wanting to go back as soon as you find a job? You get uneasy and might jeopardize your beliefs by having too much time on your hands. There is a risk that too much contemplation might confuse you. Things you liked and never questioned you start questioning now. Too many books may lead to significant doubts and potentially some cognitive dissonance.

Ideally, your contemplation should yield one of two things. It either should strongly confirm your beliefs and current path, which you will then continue to follow. Or, if you are up for new things in life and unhappy on your current path, contemplation should help you identify a few options that you should take time to explore. You might have to give yourself permission to explore those new options and not rush to the first best one. Either way, it might be useful to set yourself some deadlines to avoid drifting for too long.

Travel can be a great way to stimulate your thinking. You see other cultures and experience how others live (many with lesser means than you). You could join a monastery for some spiritual exercises. If you feel that you have a lot of contemplating to do, change scenery for a bit. Otherwise your surroundings might keep you in your current box of thinking and limit your discovery process. Travel also works wonders in meeting new people. You might get new ideas. Or you may perceive certain feelings, positive and negative, in certain situations that could give you clues to the way you should lead your life. A sunny climate might get you out of your depression and now you know that the time to move south has come. Spending time with kids doing charity work makes you want to have kids yourself...or not have them at all. Meeting a real estate agent in Uruguay gives you for the first time a jolt to explore investing in real estate at home. Meeting somebody who just opened a bed and breakfast but is honest about the hard work and loneliness of living in the countryside puts your dream of opening your own B&B away for good.

Whether you come out of this period with stronger than ever resolve about your current life path or as a changed person, you can thank your job loss. It would have been highly unlikely that you would have arrived at the same results and resolutions if you were still working full-time and worrying about your boss's demands.

MY STORY

My introspective contemplation was focused on being a first generation immigrant in the United States. I had picked this country because it offered the best opportunities and is one of the most amazing countries to live in. Unfortunately, living away from family and friends makes for long distances in travel. I asked myself "Where do I really belong? Is it time to move back after having enjoyed fantastic years? Is there a business or profession that would allow me to spend time in both countries?" I know many immigrants, no matter whether from India, Latin America, or Europe who struggle with the same issue. Even people moving within the United States to a very different region might have similar thoughts. Having time off gave me ample opportunity to confirm my choice of staying here.

14 ▪ Explore investment opportunities

After the Argentine crisis in 2001, real estate prices in the great city of Buenos Aires fell. Prices for such a world class city became even cheaper than usual when compared to other international cities. It was clear that picking up a piece of the action could be very profitable—50K could have bought you a nice one-bedroom in an upscale neighborhood. You could have purchased it and rented it out with the help of many local agencies specializing in handling foreign investors. Too bad I was working hard in New York during that year. I had no opportunity to spend time exploring this investment idea by flying down and looking at condos. No time to do research locally. No time to round up a few friends and maybe pool money for a joint investment in a small property. Sure enough, prices recovered very strongly in the subsequent years. The investment idea was the right one, but there was no way for me to have executed it.

It is not necessary to go to foreign lands. There might be a new café in your neighborhood looking for some investment. Or there might be a short sale of a small house right down the street where you live. Or say the college your son attends just hosted a competition for business ideas and you could become a small investor in a potentially lucrative venture driven by Internet-savvy students.

When you are employed, in theory, you can still pursue investment opportunities. For most of us, though, we just don't have the time to do everything at the same time. When we work, we work—this is and should be our focus. Being sidetracked would not be a good thing and we might make stupid and costly errors. We might buy badly constructed condos in Miami, go with fads (read: dot com boom), or blindly trust our friend without reading the fine print of the 400-page partnership agreement.

While you might feel more insecure without a job, you could be using your time to your advantage. You can do research. You have time to read contracts carefully. You have time to brainstorm with others regarding investment ideas. You can explore your local Chamber of Commerce to check out what is being offered. There is no shortage of opportunities to look at. If you have some savings, opportunities, big or small, could be waiting for you.

MY STORY

Given the prolonged real estate crisis, it seems to me that there should be amazing deals if you conquer your fear and have a long-term horizon. Thus I used my time to start low-bidding on some short sales, and successfully picked up a small one-bedroom condo to rent out. I had the time to do research, read books on becoming a landlord, and closed the deal at the best price per square foot in the building. Looking at Austin's great economic outlook, I am confident that the investment should pay off in the long run. I doubt I would have had the time or the focus to do this when being employed. Don't get me wrong—investing is usually no substitute for work, but once you have the time, you can use it to your advantage. Sometimes what starts out like a little occupation on the side might over time become a new career.

15 ▥ Explore career alternatives to Corporate America

Your search for your true calling (Activity #13) might have brought you to the conclusion that a career change is in store for you. You want to leave Corporate America. Now you have time to explore alternatives. There are many alternatives for you:

- Become a consultant
- Buy a franchise
- Create or join a start-up business
- Join or buy into a small or medium-sized (family) business
- Work for a non-profit entity/charity
- Go into teaching, school or college

In the current difficult economy, like in former ones, many people turn to the aforementioned options. If you consider such a move, there is a lot of help available to get you there, such as books, coaches, government programs, outplacement firms, and local small business organizations. The opportunities are endless.

I will not go into detail regarding all the options you have. There are full book shelves of material and Internet resources with much better and updated information than I could give you. You will have no trouble finding what you need. More important at this point should be the strategic thought process for you.

If you change your career, you are doing two things at the same time. First, you leave one career. Let's say you were an accountant in a big corporation. After some reflection you now want to become a church minister. You just made two decisions, not one. It is very important for you to realize that. It might be easy to decide to escape from Corporate America, but...where to? Hence, your decision should be not only a push, such as you were let go, but also a pull, something that is deeply attracting you to the new.

After many years in Corporate America, you cannot expect to know immediately what the best alternative might be for you. You have to bring both the "will" and the "skill" to charter a new course. Whether you use a coach, test ride something for a few weeks (e.g., test teaching at a summer class, work for a charity for free), you need time to do so. You now have sufficient time.

The press and magazines are full of people who are doing "second acts" and pursuing their dreams, or at least trying something new. After all, the US is the land of opportunity and optimism. Many who decided to leave Corporate America never looked back and, when interviewed, say that getting fired was the best thing that ever happened to them. Of course, there are those whose dreams got shattered and whose stories you might not find in the national press.

Only you can find out whether the lure of something different could be the real deal for you, whether you can stomach the risks, while having the energy and necessary resolve. There are many self-tests out there to help you truly assess your strengths and weaknesses. Many books show you potential strategies and how to overcome challenges. The key is, as one outplacement consultant once told me, to allow yourself time to explore. Explore the alternatives you have, and then decide which one to pick. The good news is, you are given time to explore. If you were still employed, you would never have had this time. You would have never left the company on your own; this step would have been reckless. Given that you are out of work now, this is your opportunity. Better not kill this option too early by just applying for the next available position advertised on a job board.

For example, a colleague of mine who was let go after twenty years of employment took his time and decided to buy a franchise in the service sector. He did research for several months, leveraged the outplacement firm's services, interviewed franchise organizations, decided on his favorite one, got his wife and four kids on board, and has now embarked on a new journey. He sounded quite optimistic when I talked to him with the first steps under his belt.

Everyone has different challenges when contemplating radical change. If you want to go to the non-profit sector, limited income potential might be your concern. An additional question for you might be how to preserve a comeback option, if ultimately you don't like your new choice. For others, it might be difficult to overcome mental barriers or family objections. Being perceived as somebody who downshifts—by becoming a teacher or going non-profit—can mean defending yourself in front of friends or family who think that you are throwing away your future. They will describe to you in gory detail the risks that they perceive for your new life. Overcoming these objections might be the first important hurdle for you to clear. It might streamline your arguments and thinking even more, a first test for the new path you are going to enter.

The length of time you might want to explore alternatives varies a lot. If you have no hungry kids to feed and are financially comfortable, you could easily spend up to a year exploring. A year can pass very fast and it might take you some time to test ride an idea. And why not? You are not really going to apply for a job right now, which means no explanations necessary to HR people of Corporate America. If you are financially constrained, you will probably be forced to make a decision more quickly. This is not necessarily bad, as too much time on hand may lead you to delay decision making and just drift along.

Gary Hoover, the founder of many successful companies including the famous *Hoover's Company Database* (now owned by *D&B*), and entrepreneur-in-residence at the University of Texas, thinks that "observation and travel" are part of lifelong learning, which in turn makes you a better entrepreneur. Travel gives you new ideas for a start-up. In particular, the so-called "emerging markets" have many local products that you might like. You may get ideas for importing them into the United States and make this a viable business. With regard to teaching, it might be easier for you to teach a class of English in a foreign country and get a feel for teaching than to get permission to do so in your nearby college. Joining a charity in a poor country for a while might be easier to get into (and out of) than pursuing the same here in the United States. In fact, you might even leverage the experience of your travel–charity time back home. The possibilities are virtually endless.

There is also the strategy of planning to stand on more than one leg in the future. The moment you leave Corporate America, you can mix and match, so to speak. Why not become a teacher part of the time, and a consultant the remainder? Why not join a small company three days a week to do their books as an accountant, but use the other days of the week to start your own practice? Why not explore cooking at night and teaching during the day? Maybe doing more than one thing at the same time is too risky or too demanding at the beginning, but there is nothing to stop you from aspiring to live a life where you stand on more than one leg.

MY STORY

I had a good run at Corporate America. No regrets, nothing to escape from. I also had a prior professional career as a management consultant that I am now getting back into. Leveraging my academic background by teaching some classes at a university is also in the making. This book venture came unexpectedly, but that's perfect—there is nothing better than becoming a bestselling author (well, let's see how many books I am going to sell!).

There you have it—15 amazing activities are at your disposal when you lose your job. *Part II* will broaden your understanding of why using this time strategically and not wasting it by going straight into job search is so important. Only you can decide how important this free time can be for you. Nobody is doing this for you. *Part III* and the *Appendix* will then help you implement your activities wisely and have the most unforgettable time of your life.

■ ■ ■

Part II

Strategic Use of Time at the Core of the Gift

STRATEGIC USE OF TIME AT THE CORE OF THE GIFT

A painful reminder that our time on earth is finite...

Being healthy, full of energy, and in my early forties, thoughts about potential illnesses and my own demise used to be absent. Why worry? I was not 80 years old yet! Too bad the assumption of making it to old age hit a few potholes over the last years. In early 2008 I had called Kathleen, my former girlfriend from over a decade back, when I used to live in Toronto. We had both moved on happily to be good friends with regular phone calls once or twice a year. She had a small child by then. When we talked, she let me know that she had just been diagnosed with breast cancer that had already spread all over her body. It turned out to be Stage IV, terminal. It was heartbreaking, and very disturbing.

A few months later, when my job loss became increasingly likely, Kathleen fighting cancer came to my mind while contemplating my future. Questions about the value of time, our lifetime, started nagging me. My eyes wandered more than once to the print-out of the email she had sent me. It was a little thank you note for the flowers I had sent her for encouragement after learning about her condition. Her email is to this day posted on my whiteboard as a reminder of how precious our time is. It is written by a mother with a toddler knowing that she was going to pass away in probably less than a year. You can read this email below. I did not change a single word. Whether you see the beauty and the inspiration of her message, I don't know. At least for me, it contributed to my decision to take some time off when job loss became reality.

It was not only Kathleen, though. When I looked around among friends, I saw more than one with serious health issues. One good friend survived testicular cancer (he is in his late thirties). Another had open heart surgery twice (in his early forties). Another friend had survived a very rare form of cancer in her twenties, was given no hope, but she beat the odds and is now happier than ever; another one developed the autoimmune disease lupus in her thirties.

All this was very disturbing to me. What good are all the actuarial statistics about your life expectancy, if right and left people suffer serious health problems? Of course, the statistics are right in the aggregate and statistically speaking you and I might make it to old age. Unfortunately, though, these numbers do not capture the reality of individual cases of your friends, family, or potentially one day yourself.

It is fair to say that I owe it in no small degree to Kathleen for truly opening my eyes about the value of our lifetime. Thanks to her I started to be more attentive to the difficulty of optimizing life—career, money, family, personal passions—without knowing how much time we will ultimately have.

Maybe this is not a "cool" or "fun" topic, and unusual for a career/self-help book. Nevertheless, it is a topic that nobody, not even the most successful CEO in the news, can escape from.

From: Kathleen@...
Subject: Thank you!
Date: July 10, 2008
To: MFroehls@...

Thank you for the lovely flowers, Michael. They really cheered me up! It was great to speak with you the other day. I am staying positive and finding joy and happiness in life and Liam. He is such a little boy who is the delight of my life. I hope you find what will make you happy and again never feel you do not have a choice. We create opportunities simply by thinking of choices. If we imagine it, it will come. If we do not imagine it, our life has no direction or goal to move towards. Keep imagining and dreaming, Michael, and all good things will come to you.

I look forward to your visit and catching up.

Thanks again,

Kathleen :-)

Note: My visit never happened, as her health was deteriorating fast. Only a few months later, she sold her house in Toronto to move back to her parents in Montreal. She passed away in spring 2009 at the age of 40.

INTRODUCTION

■ ■ ■

In *Part I* you have read all about the 15 activities you can elect to pursue after job loss. In light of the abundance of choices available, you might already see job loss in a different, more positive light. You might still have some doubts, though. You might still have the urge to immediately send out your résumé the moment you learn about your job loss.

It is therefore necessary to turn our discussion to the central underpinning of this book—putting your job loss in perspective to your finite time on earth. What value does the freed-up time of not having to go to work have for you? What is the upside of using this time for things outside job search for a limited period? Would you be better off that way, or rather be going immediately into job search since you always had sufficient time available for all your needs when being employed?

The goal of the following chapters is to help you get clarity on the value you attribute to time in the face of your finite life on earth. It is basically a decision between time and money for a few months.

This subject comes in two parts. First, we look at your time allocation during different phases of your life. Then, we ask whether you live life based on your expected life expectancy or based on more conservative assumptions that might include failing health and/or early death.

Important as well is the concept of opportunity costs, i.e., how much does it cost you to pursue one thing while not doing another? In our case the question is, how much do you miss out on in the job market if you delay your search? Is there even a viable option to wait for better times while reaping the benefits of pursuing some of the 15 activities? You will see why you are blessed if your job loss comes during a recession and taking time off is best to do.

OUR PERCEPTION ABOUT TIME IS OFTEN FLAWED

▩ ▩ ▩

Time is a very interesting concept, especially how we perceive and how we deal with it as human beings. As Jean-Louis Servan-Schreiber observed in his great book *The Art of Time,* there is objective time and subjective, i.e., perceived time. The first one is measured time, like an hour or a year. Subjective time is how we perceive it. Ten seconds of waiting at a red light or the ten minutes for the doctor to tell us the results of a medical test may seem like hours to us. Watching your favorite TV show may feel like minutes. Our sense of time can be distorted and this makes it hard for us to deal with time, especially planning over longer periods and for events far off in the future.

Let's take a closer look at time with regard to your job loss.

- Your total working lifetime is likely between 30 and 40 years.
- Taking three months off would represent less than 1% of that time; in other words you would still have 99% of your working life for work. If you took six months off, the number is still way below 2%, which leaves 98% for work.
- Whenever you join a company, you are making multi-year bets. Certain benefits begin only after the first year. Many retirement plans don't vest before the end of year three or even year five

99

of your employment. Non-cash compensation like stocks and options vest linearly over several years or cliff-vest after a typical three-year period. In other words, while the company can dismiss you anytime for any reason, you are making a three- or even five-year bet on your continuous employment.

If you look at the preceding different time frames, you see how insignificant a "time off" period of three or six months would be in comparison to either total work life or even the bet you make when joining a company in Corporate America. Anxiety and societal conventions make us believe how important these three or six months could be if employed, when in reality such a time period is totally inconsequential in the greater scheme of things.

TIME ALLOCATION IN VARIOUS AGES OF OUR LIFE

Let's take the concept of time a step further. Do you know how you currently allocate your time among various activities today, how it changes over your lifetime, and what your goal is in a decade or two? This question might be another eye opener.

It was a partner at a training event for young project managers at McKinsey who taught us consultants about this. He wanted us to think about how we desired to spend our time. His interest was to push all of us young and proud newly minted project managers to think a few years ahead and decide for ourselves whether spending 60–80 hours work time each week was the right path for us going forward, in particular given competing demands on time like family. His concept of thinking about time was very simple, though compelling.

First, he divided life into distinct periods, for simplicity's sake in decades (0–10, 11–20, all the way up the last bracket, age 81–death).

Second, he presented a few categories of how we can spend our waking time. I might not get the categories exactly right but the following should come close:

- *learning* (e.g., kindergarten, school, university, vocational training)
- *working* (e.g., making money, having a career, going for job satisfaction)
- *having fun* (e.g., leisure activities including travel, music, theater, games, reading)
- *dating and mating* (including courtship and sex)
- *spending time with family* (kids, parents, extended family)
- *improving our health* (e.g., going to the gym, spas, recovering from surgery)
- *doing charity work* (e.g., helping food banks, managing the finances of your local synagogue)

Third, he reminded us that you cannot spend more than 100% of your time.

Fourth, he let us reflect on if and how each decade of our life had a different pattern of spending our 100% of available time, which implies a trade-off.

Fifth, he pointed out that a certain time allocation in one decade might mean certain preparations in the previous decades. If you want to enjoy an active retirement of traveling, your preceding time most likely involves some income generating work.

Sixth and lastly, he made us think how the relative value and importance of the different categories above might be changing as we go through life. And he asked us to reflect on how we wanted the time allocation to be.

This is an exercise I would encourage you to do as well. Go back to the various decades of your past and think about the ones ahead.

Just compare our twenties, forties, and seventies for some contrast as a starting point. The following examples are just a few extremely simplified situations:

In our twenties, we most likely spend a significant portion of our time on education and work. We need to lay the groundwork for our future. Studying and working hard is our primary concern. We also spend some time on dating-mating and enjoying our leisure activities. Towards the end of the decade, we might start a family.

In our forties, educational time is probably close to zero. We devote most of our time to work and family. We are done with dating-mating and leisure activities are second to the above. We are increasing our allocation of time to healthy activities. We might get deeply involved in charity in our communities.

Fast-forward to our seventies. We are most likely done with work and are enjoying retirement. Charity and family (spending time with grandchildren) are important ways to leave our legacy behind. Taking good care of our health with daily walks, exercises in the gym, and frequent short trips to a nice climate or even a move down south have become a priority. Unless we want to fulfill a life-long dream of studying French literature or some other subject of interest to us, our time allocation for learning will be minimal.

What can you learn from this?

First, by drawing your own time allocation charts for each decade you might realize how much lifetime you still have ahead of you. This in turn should open up your eyes to how much you still can do, but also how some changes in priorities might limit certain endeavors. For example, you might start realizing that investing a lot of time in one activity like your career might be less or more appealing than you previously thought when looking at the expected changes in priorities ahead of you.

Second, you might recognize that you have not really thought about the next decades and what to do with them more than just in generic terms ("I am going to enjoy life..."). Or you already know that once you retire you will be dedicating your life to a particular charity.

The earlier you know, the better you can prepare, i.e., spending your time wisely and thinking about how to get where you want to go. You may also be shocked about how much time you have been spending on certain activities, most likely on your job vs. health, family, and leisure activities.

For how many more years do you want to keep this "time allocation"; for how many more years do you have to? Or can you even allocate more time to work given that you are recently single again, are in excellent health, and can now fully concentrate on both work and dating?

For many, a fundamental shift in thinking about life occurs at the age of 40+ for some; for others already at 30+. At that point you have some self-doubts, you have become aware of your mortality, and recognize your failed dreams and life disappointments. This shift could be triggered by a divorce or job loss, or health issues. There comes a point of self-reflection about your life, your state of happiness, and the life path you are on. Some turn to self-help or spiritual books to find answers and the encouragement to alter course. Some people change, drop, or rediscover religion. Others take a sabbatical to "find themselves." Others become depressed and start a vicious cycle of turning negative, leading to bad performance at work and at home, only to see their life surroundings getting worse by the day.

Maybe I am an optimist, but I believe the exercise about how to allocate your time during various decades of your life—past, current, desired future—can be a helpful tool to bring things into perspective and realize that our relative values that we attach to certain activities change. We might realize that certain things don't come back in life and that it is OK to change course once we get older...and wiser. It might be time to focus on different things after realizing that our needs might collide with what society or tradition expects us to do.

If you are laid off, you are given time. You can and should use this time to think. It might be unsettling at first, but you should not run away from it. Use the break to think about your time allocation—past, current, and future (desired) and what you can do to get there. This would also be one of the many ways to find your true "calling" (Activity #13), if you are in doubt.

THE RISK OF LIVING LIFE BASED ON AVERAGE LIFE EXPECTANCY

Let's now tackle the most difficult question of all: how to optimize your lifetime and your life, i.e., how to optimize your total time on earth, not knowing how long that time will be.

What to do when? Where to set priorities? What assumptions to make regarding your expected age and health?

You can spend every minute only once. You also know the saying "Yesterday is history, tomorrow is a mystery, but today is a gift, that's why it's called the 'present,'" or a variation of this sentence. It often hangs as a magnet on fridges or in cubicles at work and was most recently made famous by the movie *Kung Fu Panda*. This phrase gets right to the heart of things. History might give us good or bad memories, but it is done and gone. The future is unknown, though we can plan for it to a certain degree. Today, only the "now"—the present moment—exists.

Ideally, you can enjoy a good thing three times. The first time occurs when you plan for it, like a "once-in-a-lifetime" vacation. You plan the itinerary, look at the pretty pictures in the catalog or online, and start dreaming. The second time comes during your trip when you enjoy the vacation to the fullest. If you are lucky, your expectations are exceeded and every minute is a blessing. After your return and for the rest of your life, you look back at this special time, maybe with the help of some amazing pictures you took.

You also know the famous quote about "nobody ever regretted having not spent more time in the office during his or her life" when lying on their deathbed. In fact, let me quote right from Robert Grudin's great philosophical book *Time and the Art of Living*:

> *"How will we, five or ten or twenty years hence, look back on present time? Most probably, with envy and regret. We will envy the younger self who could, relatively speaking, do so much; and we will regret that it did not do more. We will wonder why, given youth and health, and broad reaches of time, we learned so little, loved so little, risked so little, how so much time could have drained so immemorially down the sink of routine and distraction."*[1]

[1] Robert Grudin, *Time and the Art of Living* (New York: Ticknor & Fields, 1982), 36.   **105**

Realizing that every minute is precious because once spent it does not come back, is quite powerful. It means that if you really think about it, the only thing you are short on during your life is time. Of course, health is the foundation and money might be the means to enjoy time, but it is time itself that is in short supply. In fact, it gets worse. Not only is time limited, you don't even know how much you have got left.

As I was writing the first draft of these lines, I got interrupted by a phone call. My dad was telling me that a classmate of mine just passed away at the age of 43, due to cancer. Like the passing away of my ex-girlfriend Kathleen at the age of 40, this sad event again demonstrated the important difference between the life insurance related concept of "life expectancy" and *your* personal life span.

For a life insurance company, only the average of their insured customers, their risk pool, counts. Their math is based on statistics. For example, if you are a non-smoking white male and born in 1950, you are expected to live to the age of 79, let's say.

Is this helpful to you? Yes? No? Maybe? And, if so, how exactly?

Let's analyze life expectancy together. We know that if we fall into one of the publicly available life insurance brackets, this is our mathematical expectancy. The problem is that the average numbers are not you. If you get lucky, you might outlive your life expectancy. Unfortunately, the reverse could also be true. One day, sometimes with advance warning (such as a terminal disease), sometimes without warning (car accident, heart attack), your time is up and your postmortem life is about to begin—that is, if you believe in an afterlife.

How do you optimize your life and time not knowing how long it will be? It is an unsolvable riddle. The problem is that you cannot escape the question. You still have to decide day in and day out...what do you believe? What do you do? More specifically: which of the following two "games of life" are you playing?

GAME 1: LIVE LIFE BASED ON YOUR ACTUARIAL AVERAGE LIFE EXPECTANCY

You assume you will make it to the age life insurance would tell you, based on your race, health, gender, and country you live in. In other words, you plan and live your life—investments, career, family, studies, vacation trips and everything else—with the underlying assumption that you will not die before, let's say, age 84, and likewise you will be in reasonable health up to that date.

If this is your game, you are not alone. I would argue most people in Corporate America or probably anywhere in the world are implicitly playing this game.

You work and maximize income during the regular years of employment, then retire to live the remaining years and decades happily until sudden death at 84. In this game, you feel you do not need to take any breaks from work, but rather to optimize your income based on this math; you will enjoy about 20 good years in retirement. Why would you "play" this game? It is easy to play, and does not involve much thinking. It follows the norm. Also, we are not taught any better. Finally, thinking about your own demise and analyzing circumstances that might lead you to expect a higher expected age (e.g., good family genes) or lower (e.g., emerging health issues) is for most of us no fun subject to think about.

107

GAME 2: MAXIMIZE LIFE BASED ON YOUR MINIMUM EXPECTED LIFE EXPECTANCY

▨ ▨ ▨

In this game, you want to cover your butt when it comes to making assumptions about your life expectancy. You realize that yes, if you are lucky, you may reach average life expectancy or beyond. Unfortunately, the price for being wrong is high, such as early death or a crippling disease. Ouch!

Just because the average of all people of your gender, age, race, and health, indicates that you should make it to 84 does not mean you will make it. Draw a comparison with the stock market. Yes, stocks on average might increase 8% per year, but the stock you own might go down to zero, if the company goes belly up. Since you are not putting all of your financial assets into the stock market based on its expected average gains, why would you do the same with your most precious asset, your lifetime? Not a good idea...but how to manage? Maybe the hippies in the 1960s had it right after all. They enjoyed life day by day (at least for a while), not worrying about the future.

On the other hand, if you do make it to 84, you might be poor because you enjoyed your life a bit too much after joining the latest gurus in India and not thinking about the future and how to make a living long term. Where is the balance? What can you do?

SHALL I PLAY GAME 1 OR GAME 2? HOW TO PLAY GAME 2?

▨ ▨ ▨

It is exactly because of the daunting task of playing Game 2 that most of us just resort to Game 1. We capitulate and go back to the easier (though still not easy) math and trade-offs of Game 1, despite seeing every day the diseases and death of people around us who may be younger than us. I am sorry to tell you that I don't have the solution for you either. Only you can decide which game to play and then, how to play it. It all depends on your personal risk tolerance. As an optimist, you might play Game 1. If you are more of a realist or pessimist, you should opt for Game 2.

But how do you play Game 2? How do you play defensively without giving up too much upside or the risk of outliving your financial means?

As with all good decision making, understanding the issue and having transparency about the choices is the first step forward. I hope to have already helped you with that.

Second, eliminate time wasters like spending time with "false friends." What I mean by "false friends" or "fair weather friends" is spending time with those who are only your friends because you happen to live in the right neighborhood but who forget about you the moment your economic situation changes.

Third, realize what employment means vs. self-employment. Employment means that you are renting a significant portion of your working lifetime to a third party, a corporation. You rent out your time for receiving compensation in return. When you are renting your time to a corporation, make sure that this asset in short supply is getting fair compensation. It will not come back. You are just trading it for some immediate benefits (having money to buy shelter, food, and clothes) and, if you save, some future benefits (being able to buy shelter, food, and clothes later in your life).

Fourth, don't put all your "time eggs" into one basket. Take vacations regularly, spend time with family, and diversify your time allocation early on. Instead of maximizing your career (time egg basket "money"), earn a bit less, and spend more time on your time egg basket "family." Think about any bonus lost or promotion lost as a premium for an insurance policy called "regret policy of not having spent enough time on XYZ." Also, take "mini-retirements" as the bestselling author of *The 4-Hour Workweek*, Timothy Ferris, calls them. Many companies offer paid or unpaid leaves of absence after a certain number of years of service. These opportunities are like little insurance policies on a short life or early deterioration of health.

It is therefore surprising that society has it a bit wrong. Since everybody is in the same boat of maximizing lifetime and deciding on Game 1 vs. Game 2, wouldn't it be in everybody's interest to organize the middle years of our life a bit differently? What I mean is that after working 15 to 20 years and reaching 40 +/- (after having saved some money and still being in decent health), wouldn't it be better to take a year off and add the "missing" year of working life to the end instead of working without interruption and hoping for the best at 65 and beyond?

The good news is that you don't have to wait for society to revolutionize and reach such a utopian state of enlightenment. Just take the opportunity when it is handed to you on a golden platter...when you are laid off! All 15 activities—the 7 no-regret and the 8 optional ones—are at your disposal.

OPPORTUNITY COSTS AND THE OPTION TO WAIT

■ ■ ■

Our discussion about time and your analysis of your personal situation should have led you by now to a "yes/no" decision with regard to accepting the gift of job loss. Either you value more highly the freed-up time and the chance of pursuing many of the 15 activities than immediate job search or you don't. Since you weigh job/money with mostly non-monetary items (e.g., dream vacation, family time), there is no formula, no easy math you can apply. It is like comparing food with furniture or a car with a vacation. You pick what is more valuable to you in the circumstances. It is your life; hence, whatever you decide is perfect.

If you are, however, still undecided, maybe two additional time-related economic concepts can help you. The first one is the concept of "opportunity costs," the question of what you miss out if you do or don't do a certain activity.

The second concept is the "option to wait." This is just a fancy way of saying that by postponing something, you hope that you will be better off later.

Let's apply these concepts to job search; we'll start with a simplified example:

The financial service industry shed over 100,000 jobs in New York City alone during the Great Recession. Banks were hit the hardest. They all announced hiring stops. Nevertheless, usually smart people who were let go immediately tried finding jobs against all odds in banks in New York. Did this make sense? No, it did not. If there are no jobs available (or the probability of finding one is extremely low), it means that whether you are looking for a job or not is irrelevant. Expressed differently, you could have gone to the beach during that time...or pursued the 15 activities we talked about. Had you kissed New York good-bye for a while, your opportunity costs of doing your dream vacations or whatever you fancied would have been very low. You would not have missed anything at home. Six months later, you still would have no job, but you would have experienced six great months doing what you wanted to do. Those who stayed in New York would likely not have found employment in their hard-hit industry. They would be stressed out and probably not have had a great time. The opportunity cost of looking for a job against all odds was high. They could not do anything else and still did not achieve what they wanted to achieve.

In other words, opportunity cost analysis means you compare two mutually exclusive actions on your part and try to gauge in advance which one is preferable.

You can also compare one action with that action further down the road. Do it now vs. do it later. Search for a job now vs. search for it later. Let's go back to the example above. Instead of comparing the expected benefits and costs of job search today with going to the beach, you could compare the benefits and costs of a job search today with a job search later. How much later? You should compare with a date that makes economic sense. We know that recessions usually last less than a year, though their duration can vary a lot; this current downturn is unusually severe. Normally, if you lose your job in a recession, you might want to think 9–12 months ahead because history tells you that likely the economy will have improved by then. You bet that by delaying job search you will be better off. Better off could mean finding a job vs. not finding one or keeping the old salary level vs. taking a pay cut by taking the first best offer. Of course, there are no guarantees either way, and you have to decide which side of the bet to take.

If you now compare job loss during a boom and a recession, you come to interesting results (again keeping it simple). Assuming that you lose your job in either period, would you rather accept the gift of job loss in a boom or in a recession? I am using the term recession in a sense that you would have a much harder time of finding a job than in boom times. If the economy is doing great in your profession, but the country is in depression, for the sake of this discussion you would live in boom times.

If your answer is "recession," you are right (focusing only on the economic situation and assuming everything else would be equal for you). The opportunity costs of not looking for a job for a while would be low, and the value of the option to wait would be high, since you expect the recession to end eventually. You are not missing anything, and you are not paying a price for waiting for better times.

In boom times, the situation is the reverse. Not going immediately back into the labor market after job loss can cost you dearly financially. You could have earned good money, but you did not because you took time off. Even worse, given that busts follow booms, the option to wait carries zero or even negative value for you, because you have the risk of reentering the work force during a recession. Thus, during a boom, it is more expensive for you to accept the gift compared to a recession. Be careful, though, not to reject the gift outright. The trade-off of optimizing lifetime vs. money still holds. Neither the concept of "opportunity costs" nor of the "option to wait" helps you with that.

In summary, to make your decision about the acceptance or rejection of the gift of job loss, you have to get clarity on the value of time in light of your mortality. You can then supplement your analysis by looking at the opportunity costs of your potential decision and assess the economic benefits and costs of delaying your job search, waiting for better times to come.

▦ ▦ ▦

Part III
Making the Most out of Your Gift

MAKING THE MOST OUT OF YOUR GIFT

January 2010—a job interview on Park Avenue, New York City, in the office of a global search firm

"I took a look at your résumé, Michael. It seems like I do not have your latest version in front of me."

"You have the latest version, Bob," I answered with a confident, but probably somewhat forced smile "because I took some time off to realize a few of my lifelong dreams. I took what some might call a sabbatical."

Here I was in a suit and tie and engaging in my first job interview for a long time. What would I encounter? Astonishment? Envy? Lack of comprehension? Revulsion at daring to escape New York instead of actively looking for the next job? How to convince a headhunter that after being laid off in a recession, the best thing you can do is to realize some of your dreams, learn new things, and perhaps come back for an even better career after the recovery of the economy should be under way? How to convey that my time off was a well-analyzed business decision, not a mid-life crisis? How to explain the expected benefits, the tremendous upside, and

117

the lack of inherent risk, within a few minutes to somebody who might have never thought about taking time off...and was now about to make a decision whether or not to present me as a candidate to his client?

Bob paused for a few seconds. Probably he was not sure how to react.

"Good for you" he said, a bit unsure, "what did you do during the last months?"

"Well, I had three major goals, like a good consultant always has. First of all, I wanted to visit those places in South America where I had not been during the last years, either for business or pleasure. I used my time off to visit Colombia, Peru, Uruguay, and the Andes region of Argentina and Chile. It was for pleasure, but also to deepen my knowledge about this growth region for career purposes.

Second, I wanted to do a few things that I might not be able to do later in my life. Call it my "bucket list." For example, I accompanied my 74-year-old mom to the country where she was born and had not been back for 64 years. We spent real quality time together. I also hiked the Inca Trail in Peru. This trekking adventure takes place in high altitude. Who knows whether I would have the health to do so in my 50s or 60s? I visited the famous ancient Mayan sites of Copán in Honduras and Tikal in Guatemala, temples and pyramids in Egypt, and the spectacular desert city Petra in Jordan.

Who knows when the next civil or real war will break out and close the borders? In fact, almost to prove my point, I visited Copán during a presidential coup right before the borders were closed, though luckily only temporarily. Better enjoy these ancient cities while you can!

My third and last goal was getting my Spanish language skills up to true proficiency. It had always bothered me that I had been working with Latin America, but never spoke this language fluently. There had never been enough time to learn it while being employed. Finally last year, I took immersion classes and passed an internationally recognized language exam.

My time off was rewarding in other aspects as well. I learned about being a landlord and bought my first little short sale unit to rent out. The best of all, however, was that I met my new girlfriend on a small plane into the jungle of Guatemala. We have great plans for our future," I finished my explanation with excitement.

During my little monologue, I kept looking at Bob for any reaction. His face had warmed up considerably. "Michael, this is amazing. I wish that I could have done that. The last year was not a bad year for me, but I always had wished to do what you just did."

"Let me add something," I said, "I think my time off after losing my job was the best counter-cyclical investment I have ever made in my life. It takes three things to do this: some time, decent health, and a bit of money, though not much. The problem is: when you are young, you usually have health and time, but no money. When you are old, you might have money and time, but who knows what your health will be? And in all the time in between, you might have money and health, but no time since you are working. Last year, like in every other recession, remember, decent jobs were scarce. In more financial terms, my opportunity costs were virtually zero. I would probably not have found a good job at all, at least not during the first half of the year. And on the other side of the equation, travel was cheap. Heck, I even made it into a very high level of American Airlines' frequent traveler program, just by flying economy class."

"Well, Michael, I think that you should meet our client. I will keep you posted. My assistant will contact you for scheduling interviews."

INTRODUCTION

■ ■ ■

You see the proverbial writing on the wall and now you are probably only weeks or months away from losing your job. Or you have just now been let go. Now what? How do you turn your agonizing situation into an amazing time of your life? You have decided to accept the gift of free time. Now you have to implement it.

Let's turn our attention to the 12 most important questions you might have. Not all will apply to you. Read the ones that interest you and skip the rest.

OVERVIEW

THE 12 MOST IMPORTANT QUESTIONS

1. Do I need goals for my post-employment time? What activities should I select?

2. How much time should I plan to take off before starting my job search?

3. How should I schedule my selected activities? Is there a perfect sequence?

4. Should I plan everything ahead or decide as I'm moving along?

5. How do I deal with potential financial constraints?

6. How do I deal with potential family constraints?

7. What do I tell my family, friends, and the business community about my decision to accept the gift of job loss? How do I position myself upon return?

8. How can I optimize my travel experience, realize my "bucket list," and keep lasting memories?

9. How can I best check out a different location to work and live?

10. How can I best check out a new career outside of Corporate America?

11. How deeply should I stay in touch with the job market while enjoying my time off?

12. When do I know that I should start my job search and end my time off, concluding my gift of job loss?

1 ▨ **Do I need goals for my post-employment time? What activities should I select?**

The 7 no-regret activities should be your baseline, the activities you do no matter what. Your selection among the 8 optional activities depends on the personal goals that you set for yourself.

What will be the one, two, or three goals for your time off?

It could be just one big item such as a two-month dream vacation to Australia. It could be a combination of learning something new and donating time to charity. You might just mix and match vacations with checking out a new city to live and work. You plan to spend four weeks in a European monastery to find your true "calling" before investing the subsequent months to implement your findings. Alternatively, you stay home with your family, but dedicate time to explore real estate investment opportunities in your community.

I strongly encourage you to set goals. The more precise they are, the better. For example, if you want to get some education, determine upfront what degree or level you want to reach. If you want to get into shape, clarify how much weight loss or muscle mass you would like to achieve. If you want to check out a different location, plan how you will do that and what your decision points will be.

Setting goals and having achieved them is also good as proof of your discipline when you re-enter the job market. You can frankly talk about them. Furthermore, during the time of implementing them, they always serve as guideposts.

I am not advocating that you should write a business plan for your time off or get too bogged down in details, but setting out a course is much easier when you know what you want to get out of it. Goals are important for you to know where you are going. You want to avoid looking back later and feeling that you wasted your precious time off.

After having set your goals and priorities, you will have to match them with the time it will take to realize these goals and with the realities of financing your time off. There might also be other constraints because of children or health issues. You might now enter an iterative process until you have found your best plan for the time ahead. Nevertheless, keep some flexibility and don't assume that everything has or will go according to plan.

Just remember, taking time off should not be a defensive escape from the past but the embracing of something very special and potentially new.

2 ▪ How much time should I plan to take off before starting my job search?

We human beings are attached to round numbers. For us, chunks of time come in months, quarters, and years. In order to make it easy, I would consider three months, six months, or a year for your active time off, i.e., the duration you do not focus on job search. The length of time will depend on your goals, your personal situation including your finances, and your overall atti-tude towards risk.

If you have never taken time off and don't know what a vacation of even two weeks is like, three months might be all you need. If you are well organized, three months can give you lots of opportunities. It is also a short enough period of time that nobody will notice your absence, in case you are concerned about taking too much time off before looking for a job.

Taking six months might be the ideal timeline for many. This time span allows for pursuing several of the optional activities and to do a broad-based sweep of things you always wanted to do. For example, you could do a bike trip in Utah for three weeks, come back, and then head off to Mexico to learn Spanish in a six-week immersion class eight hours a day. After this educational period, you take a week to travel with your dad to Normandy where he gloriously fought in 1944. Add a week of respite in between your trips and you have still more than three months to spend. Plenty of time to look at investment opportunities, check out a new location for a new career, and do some meaningful charity work.

Six months is also a good time to bridge a bad job market in an average recession. You take advantage of the low opportunity costs. You don't miss anything while being away. If you did your analysis of your industry, city, and economy overall, you will have a good feeling for the employment trend in your field of expertise.

There is no need to be rigid about your timing. Once you have had enough, maybe after four months into your six month plan, you may feel that you are done and can move on to job search.

Taking a year off is the grand-daddy of all. This is your option if you want to seriously catch up on travel or want to explore a different career or learn something new that might take several months. Twelve months might also allow you to allocate some time to reconnect with some old and lost friends, or organize a reunion of "old buddies."

The arguments for a one-year time frame are easy. Since you are taking time off anyhow, why not go "all in" and get it all done—your whole "bucket list." Since you are a hard worker you know that no matter what kind of job you will return to, you will be dedicated for at least a few years. The current opportunity will not come back for a long stretch. A year might also be fantastic in a deep recession like the current one, when you are not missing anything by going away and enjoying alternatives to a potentially frustrating job search. Sometimes waiting for the opportune timing is the right thing to do and nothing to be ashamed of. Moreover, when you have to explain to a hiring manager your motivation for taking a year off vs. six months, where is the difference?

Another way to think about the length can be in terms of time ranges. At the low end, how much time do you need to get the most pressing things done? At the high end, how much time would you need to implement everything on your list, or when would you not feel comfortable continuing anymore? You might decide to plan three months for now, but have your mind set to extend by three additional months, if you realize that this is not enough. For example, you might decide to learn French in Quebec only to discover that you need more time to check out the job market after you mastered French reasonably well.

Some flexibility and planning of "bonus time" is also needed. Your kids might have unexpected demands for your attention or a trip you scheduled with your spouse needs to be postponed because of sudden conflicts with your spouse's work.

3 ▪ How should I schedule my selected activities? Is there a perfect sequence?

First things come first. This means that you should do the 7 no-regret activities first. This might take you six to eight weeks at least. It will be a great foundation for the remainder of your time

125

off. The list of these seven activities in *Part I* is listed in recommended order, but you can pick them to your liking. As outlined earlier, if you see the ax coming your way, you should start working on some of these activities as early as possible even before lay-off to save time.

With regard to travel, one factor to consider is when your travel partner or partners will be available. If you travel with your spouse and children, you will have to coordinate with their schedules; if you travel with friends, you'll need to organize it with them. Hence, you will have to be a bit opportunistic and open to compromise. If you are traveling alone, then it's all up to you.

One important factor to keep in mind is that any travel destination has several tourist seasons. There is high season, usually during local school vacation time, when prices are high and places are crowded. While you would expect the climate to be the best at this time, this is not necessarily the case. Many places are much better to visit right before or after high season, when the weather is great, prices lower, and no crowds to be seen. For example, if you want to visit Florida, you could go in the expensive high season (December until April), or the adjacent season, May until November, to have a much better and cheaper experience.

The only other constraints might be dates you cannot move. You have to file your tax return by April 15, unless you extend your filing date; this means some preparation before that deadline. There could also be important birthdays in your family, your kids' school year, or certain medical appointments that you already scheduled. It is smart to leverage these days as anchor points for being home and working with them rather than seeing them as roadblocks.

4 ▓ **Should I plan everything ahead or decide as I'm moving along?**

Depending on your personality, you might be more or less comfortable with planning everything, nothing, or partially ahead. There is no right or wrong. A combination usually works best.

Some books on sabbaticals advise you to plan ahead one month for every month of travel or month of sabbatical. This is utter nonsense. Think about what the drivers of planning really are. They are money (often better discounts when booking ahead), immunizations and visas (depending on where you go), and cases where early reservations are advisable in sought-after places. There is not much more to it. You can purchase travel health insurance online on short notice. Getting local money via ATMs is now possible even in some of the most remote locations on earth. Your valid passport should be in your hands anyhow. If you go away for long, you will have to arrange for bills to be paid (best done automatically), mail boxes to be emptied and plants to be watered (ask friends, family, or neighbors), and that is it. There are also pet services in case you travel for some time and cannot take your pets with you.

Of course, if you apply to a school or vocational program, there are lead times and application deadlines that you have to respect. These times between the application and the start date could be great opportunities to pursue the other activities.

5 ▓ **How do I deal with potential financial constraints?**

Your initial reaction to the ideas in this book probably was: "I can't do it, I don't have the money." While this could be indeed the case, chances are that this reflex does not stand up to closer scrutiny. You are richer than you think you are.

If you forget the fear caused by job loss for a moment, you might realize that you have plenty of money to survive the next months or even a year or two. One reason for fear could be that the financial industry, self-serving, always talks about our "financial gaps." Or you see neighbors with a bigger home and conclude that your own savings and net worth are deficient. I would speculate that most readers are neither millionaires nor independently wealthy, nor so poor as not to be able to live for a few months without employment income. Moreover, if you lose your job, you might get severance, unemployment benefits, and money from vested stocks. You also have savings or securities that provide some income or can be liquidated. There is also the family, from parents who could help to your spouse. If you look closely, things may not look that bad.

We talked about the mandatory financial house cleaning as one of the no-regret activities to do (Activity #5). Most likely, a bit of downsizing would come in handy as well. Besides getting a professional financial expert to help you, there are good self-help tools available. For example, I highly recommend a subscription to *Money Magazine* and the *Wall Street Journal* series of personal financial guides. They are easy reads and give extremely practical advice. With regard to planning and financing your sabbatical, there are two books I find useful: *Power Sabbatical* by Robert Levine and *Escape 101* by Dan Clements & Tara Gignac.

Most of the 15 activities advocated are not very expensive (except going back to school). They take time but not a lot of money. They demand a bit of ingenuity. Instead of going to Paris, go to Buenos Aires (one fourth of the cost); instead of learning Spanish in Spain, pick Guatemala (one tenth of the cost); travel in off-season (40% off); optimize frequent flyers miles, take advantage of specials, and fly mid-week; where possible, stay with friends and family; cancel cable at home and watch TV in the gym; get rid of costly data plans for the latest gadgets and avoid roaming charges. The list could go on.

No matter where you live, there are many reasonable options close to home. You can take Spanish classes in your home town or via *Skype*. You can go hiking probably very close to where you live. You can study in the local library and take advantage of free or cheap continuing education classes. You can get involved in your favorite charity in your town. You can take week-end trips by bus or train to see cities of interest to you.

Some authors propose financing longer overseas travel by finding some temporary work. Typical advice is to teach English abroad. This might work for some of you. You have to decide whether the complexity of getting a work permit (you do not want to work "undocumented") and the little money you earn for these stints warrant the complexity of this undertaking. Personally, I would rather shorten the length of my time off by prioritizing my activities than diluting the experience by doing work that I usually would not do. On the other side, if teaching could be one of your passions, becoming a certified teacher for English as a second language (ESL) and finding a school for a test ride could be perfect.

Some authors recommend going into debt to pay for a longer time off, if necessary. Admittedly, I can see the rationale in the context of my arguments—a bit of debt should not be a roadblock for a great once-in-a-lifetime opportunity. I still hesitate to recommend debt. It is counter to my belief that no consumer

129

expense ever should be financed by debt. It would also contradict the idea of getting your financial house in order (Activity #5).

There is a small grey area. If you use debt for education or to get a degree or to test the waters for a new career, you are making an investment in your future. If you do a bit of travel around your educational activity, there is nothing wrong with it. For example, if you have a clear indication that your program management qualifications are sought in Montréal, Quebec, but you lack the advanced French language skills and are a bit short on cash (e.g., it is tied up in your illiquid home), taking a small loan to finance eight weeks of intense French classes plus maybe a little vacation to see Quebec should be OK. On the other hand, going on a 180-day cruise around the world financed by credit card debt without any knowledge what to do after the cruise would be reckless (with the exception of doing such a trip when you or your partner is threatened by a terminal illness). If your parents gave you the money as a first installment of their inheritance, you should welcome it. In that case you are spending family money and not going into debt.

In summary, analyze your financial situation coolly, and then decide what you can do and for how long. Take a look at your savings including severance, at the many choices you have to reduce costs, and evaluate the range of activities you can do cheaply or for free. Don't hesitate to use some help. Just be cautious when it comes to consumer debt. It is something you generally should avoid.

6 ▪ **How do I deal with potential family constraints?**
Apart from citing financial issues, having a spouse with or without children or children without a spouse could be the other knee-jerk reaction to reject any thought about accepting the gift

of job loss. Just to be clear, I am not talking about hardship situations where crippling health issues of family members or taking care of aging parents and other obligations can be real obstacles. I am talking about the normal "spouse" or "family with kids" scenario.

Let's first talk about the case of having a spouse, but no kids. We can further distinguish a non-working spouse from a working spouse. If you have a non-working spouse, the same logic to financing time off applies as being single—no difference: either you can afford it or you cannot (see above). You can do the same cost saving moves whether you are single or a couple.

If your spouse works, (s)he could be a financial help to your time off; you are much better off than any single. If there are no financial roadblocks, the question for a couple then becomes the coordination of time. If (s)he lets you go alone or has time to go with you, perfect. If (s)he does not want you to go, you might have to use your negotiation skills to find a compromise...but getting agreement with your spouse is beyond the topic of this book! Of course, if you have neglected your marriage during years of hard work, now might be the time to stay home and spend as much quality time together as possible (Activity #7).

Now let's enter children into the picture. The only real issue we are talking about is extended travel. Many activities (e.g., doing charity, learning something new, spending a few weeks away to check out a new location) you can perform close to home without any impact on your kids. With regard to travel, things depend a bit on your kids' age. Many parents take babies and toddlers with them. Home schooling for long-term travel is one option (just read *One Year Off* by David Elliot Cohen, or *World*

Trek by Russell and Carla Fisher; none of them come across as risk seeking or as neglecting their children—in fact Cohen is an accomplished bestselling author). Maybe grandparents or neighbors can supervise your kids for a while and you reciprocate at a different time. If this is not an option, focus on doing more things in your region with day trips or short overnight stays. Lastly, if you were used to extended business travel before, ask yourself, would travel for your own good be any different in terms of being away from home?

Despite any family constraints you might have, I am optimistic that you still have countless options to pick from. Enough choices not just to default immediately back to the "let-me-just-apply-for-the-next-job-here-no-matter-anything-else" option.

7 ▪ What do I tell my family, friends, and the business community about my decision to accept the gift of job loss? How do I position myself upon return?

When you start out, tell them the truth, simply the truth. Explain your reasoning, your motivation. Make them read this book. There is no reason to be defensive, to lie, or make stuff up. You say it as it is. Don't ask for permission, since jealous people or those with their own agendas and fears might try to stop you. Tell them *after* your decision and after your first non-cancelable trip is booked and paid for.

Positioning after your time off should not be too difficult either. You probably learned new things. You demonstrated you have a grown-up personality, and showed project skills organizing your time off. Some sabbatical books suggest you do charity work such that you can market it later.

These soft skills might be important, but if you are concerned about having "something to show for it," you would be better off coming back with some job relevant hard skills. This could be a degree, a certificate, or the acquisition of deep cultural and business knowledge of a country through charity work, or experience in start-ups where you are now a board member.

How far you want to concern yourself with your marketing story before or during your time off is your decision. I believe you can always craft a story after the fact that is genuine. As long as you have a rationale and convey the passion of what you did, you should not have any issues. You were not watching TV for months but actively pursued various activities. Don't worry too much during your time off, or even worse, restrict your activities upfront just because somebody from HR one day might be questioning you about why you did A and not B.

8 ▩ How can I optimize my travel experience, realize my "bucket list," and keep lasting memories?

Travel is one of the most important benefits your time off may offer. It might be literally now or never to travel for several weeks uninterrupted, be it for fun, education, charity, quality time with family, or testing a new location to work and live.

▩ Selecting travel destinations

When it comes to picking a destination, the world is really your oyster...subject to your financial restrictions, time constraints, and any visa barriers. Look at your goals and activities for your time off, including your "bucket list," then take out the globe and get started.

133

If you are overwhelmed by choices, go to any bookshop and take a peek in the General Travel section. You can spend a few hours there and will have plenty of ideas afterwards. You will find excellent books by *Rough Guides* and *Lonely Planet*. They list the top 50 or 100 destinations worldwide based on various characteristics. The descriptions and amazing pictures will make you want to leave immediately. Moreover, talk to friends and family about the unforgettable places they have visited.

Since you may have some financial constraints, one trick is to think in alternative destinations. Everything on earth exists more than once; it is just named differently and differently priced. You can pick the alternative that is cheaper. Fly to Buenos Aires, where the dollar is extremely strong, to get inspired by early 20th century architecture and European flair. Forego visiting expensive Paris, where the dollar is weak. Tan at close-by beaches in Florida instead of far away Hawaii, if you live on the East coast, and do the opposite if you live on the West coast. Learn French in easy-to-reach Quebec instead of far-away France. Climb the Rockies instead of the Alps; do horseback riding in Arizona instead of Chile.

Look at exchange rates, local safety, synergies of traveling to multiple destinations, pick places where friends live...there are many options. You won't be able to see the whole world anyhow.

▪ Deciding on the lengths of trips

In terms of the lengths of your trips, I suggest that you don't travel for more than a few weeks without having a break and coming home. When you read travelogues, it sounds like a dream to leave home and be away for months exploring the world, the wilderness, the oceans, and everything else. Reality is different, though. Many would say that after two or three months, travel fatigue sets in. Even worse, things might start to look alike. It is much better to come home after an extraordinary trip, relax for a few days, and let the experience and impressions settle in. You then can also deal with all the items at home that need attention (going through the mail, catching up with friends, checking job boards, etc.).

▦ *Managing your home while away*

Very important: never ever be without a home or place to return to and feel comfortable. Many travelogues talk at length about subletting or selling your place before going away for a few months or longer. I think that this is a bad idea. Pursuing various activities after lay-off requires you to have a home base. The home base could be a second home you move into or a smaller unit instead of the big one you lived in before. There is nothing wrong with downsizing and saving some money. Or if you have a three-bedroom place, you could sublet one room for a while. You can even move in with Mom if she has a big home. What I am cautioning you against is to have no home base at all. First, no job and no home can be very unsettling. Second, it takes time to move out, store, find a new place, and move in again. Way too stressful. This might be fine if you already have a job lined up after your time of travel, but for any other situation it would be very inconvenient and almost reckless. You want to be able to return fast, if you get the magic call for the dream job that you did not expect. After two months you might feel that the time has come to test the job market a bit before continuing with your list of activities. In either case, you need a home base.

I understand that keeping a home while traveling for a long time might add to your costs. Nevertheless, you should cut down on travel or do more near-distance activities rather than give up your home.

▪ *Choosing group travel vs. individual travel*

Many people without much travel experience opt automatically for group travel. Especially when traveling abroad they believe in "safety in numbers." There is the convenience of everything being organized and tours led in English. Going with a group sometimes comes at a steep price. First, you usually pay more than doing it individually (the only exception being some beach resorts where charter tours get better rates by buying large contingents). Second, you have limited freedom. When the group moves on, you move on. You want to stay an hour extra in the museum? Too bad. You want to see another castle along the Rhine River that is not on the program? Too bad. You don't like your tour guide for the ten-day trip? Too bad.

There are instances, though, when group travel is a great bet. If you never traveled abroad and have no travel experience, starting with group travel might be the right choice for you. Sometimes, travel destinations mandate or strongly encourage groups. Here we are talking either certain countries with non-democratic regimes, or national parks and wilderness areas where groups can get easier trekking permits than individuals. Group travel might also be better if there are security problems on the ground or any other issues that make individual travel not practical or economical.

Individual travel can be fun to prepare, and even more pleasurable to do. You can mix and match your choice of hotels. Instead of going with a group that only stays in one class of hotels, you can pick five-star hotels in the big cities, but beach huts near the ocean. Individual travel also allows you to leverage group travel at the point of destination. You can rent a local guide or join a local tour. Individual travel is also better to get to know the locals. By picking your own restaurants and negotiating your own way, you come automatically in contact with locals and other tourists. Most destinations are safe, people speak some English, and places are easy to navigate. If you get lost, it will be an additional experience to write home about. Don't think that only the US has good roads to navigate. Many countries have equal or even better infrastructure, which makes driving your rental car a lot of fun.

▨ *Traveling with a spouse, friends, and alone*

Should you travel with friends, your spouse, or go alone? I was fortunate to have done all of the above. A spouse is great for fun vacations or if you are on the same wavelength with regard to the way you like to travel. Travel with spouse and/or kids offers you important quality family time. Travel with one or several friends is great to reconnect, have a more party-like atmosphere, or pursue activities your spouse might not like (e.g., specialized sports). Travel alone can be the most rewarding one. It forces you to spend time with yourself. It gives you time to think that you usually don't have. It forces you to meet other people to interact with. What might be strange at the beginning can be extremely satisfying over time. You are exploring something new every day and nobody is stopping your rhythm. I recommend that at least once you travel alone. Whether it is a weekend in a different city, a few long strolls along the beach, or a week spent in a monastery. That is the only true time you have with your-self, the only time of not being interrupted during your thinking about your future. It is the only time you have without the literal and figurative noise around you.

■ Leveraging travel for finding business and investment opportunities

Ideas move across borders. Especially the emerging markets in Asia and Latin America have fashion brands, food chains, technology concepts, and service ideas that you might encounter during your travel. You might fall in love with a product and decide to start importing it to the US. Or you see that a certain location has no appealing language schools. You stay there and start one (as did a Swiss woman in Buenos Aires).

Absorbing new ideas during travel is very valuable. Whether your travel is international or within the US, most good ideas start somewhere local. This could be your chance.

■ Keeping lasting memories from your travel

The first thing that comes to mind is taking pictures. If you take pictures, you might enlarge them at home or convert them into a nice table book that will last forever. It would become a con-versation starter when your friends, family, and neighbors are over for dinner.

You have a few more choices to make your memories stick.

First, little magnets are great souvenirs. These little items are sometimes beautifully designed; sometimes almost ugly...it does not matter. Before I open my fridge, I spot a magnet and stop for a second to remember my past trips. I have collected magnets from all over the world. It is one of cheapest and best ways to preserve your memory.

Second, I reserve one layer of a huge bookshelf for kitsch from around the world. Well, not really kitsch, but little items that you cannot call art. It is quite a collection by now: a little Mao clock from Shanghai, a little toy llama from Peru, porcelain cows from Switzerland, a wooden elephant from India, a tango dancing couple made of clay from Buenos Aires, and a little Moai stone figure from Easter Island. One piece alone may look like kitsch, but they all together look very, very cool!

My third idea relates to those of you who like maps and other collectibles on your trip. For whatever reasons, maps, old and new, attract our attention. That's why many people have a globe. If you go hiking or visit a national park, you might get a map or buy one. Framing a map or a piece of it and putting it up on the wall is always a nice memory and a cheap way of decorating empty walls. Same goes for dinner menus, advertisements for concerts, wine labels, boat tickets—they all look great if put up on the wall behind glass.

My favorite travel souvenir is art. This could be paintings, sculptures, or professional photographs. I bought an old historic photograph of Montevideo's harbor for $5 and little aquarelles of the tango neighborhood in Buenos Aires for $25. For $50 I acquired a painted bed sheet that depicts centuries-old stone carvings in the Chilean Andes. I brought home a steel sculpture created from a modern artist in Cusco, Peru, for about $700.

If you have pictures and other collected items at home, your trips and time off will always stay with you. Nobody will ever be able to take your memories away. Unlike the job you lost.

9 ▨ **How can I best check out a different location to work and live?**

If you feel that your career has come to a dead end with no hope of improvement, you have to take a look at both the industry and location you are in. If your city is doing fine, but your industry is not, you might find something in a new industry. If you like your industry but your city is doing badly, consider moving. After you do your analysis and come up with one or several alternatives to live as proposed in *Part I* (Activity #11), you need to go there and see whether these are real alternatives.

The best way to explore a new location is staying with a friend, friend of a friend, or family. You have immediate access to local knowledge and infrastructure. Moreover, your host has neighbors and business contacts that are most likely happy to answer questions from somebody who would make them proud by picking "their" city to relocate to. You can use any business contacts, social media networks, and just walk around to those places that might interest you. Get a feel for the location, the traffic, the weather, the infrastructure, the people, the school situation, and living expenses.

Ask yourself whether you would like to live there, and if so, whether the chances of finding a job might be higher than at home. If the location you picked is in a foreign country, take the time to familiarize yourself with the visa process, the tax situation, and any particularities of the place. Take a few weeks to get your language skills up to date, in case you chose a country where English is not spoken. Spend time in coffee shops and talk to random people. Check out the cultural and sports scene. Where are the neighborhoods you would like to live if you moved?

Be honest with yourself—does the reality match your expectations? Are you there only because it is that bad at home or do you feel attracted to the place? Ideally, you would like to be in the new place not just as a refugee because you feel you are being pushed out of the old.

Enjoy the discovery process. No matter what the final outcome might be, you have widened your horizon by getting to know a new place. If you decide to change your location for good, go ahead and apply for a job or whatever you want to do. If you decide to let the option of moving pass, be happy as well. You made a decision based on facts.

10 ▪ How can I best check out a new career outside Corporate America?

If your "calling" means exploring options outside Corporate America, for example in teaching, non-profit, or start-up, you probably have an idea or passion for something. There is no shortage of literature and opportunities out there. My advice would be to test things out first before committing, as you would do with a new location before moving for good. Don't just jump.

If you want to check out teaching, hold a few guest lectures, teach a summer class at an open enrollment school, or ask the college or graduate school where you received your degree if you could teach just one class. Don't change too many variables at once. Ideally conduct your test run in or next to the city you currently reside in or find a safe opportunity during a limited stay in a foreign country.

If you are exploring non-profit, you might consider an unpaid multi-week internship or a paid project before signing up in order to get to know the new place. The world is littered with former employees from Corporate America who naively went into the non-profit sector only to run screaming in the other direction a short time later. They could not handle the politics and personalities of those in charge who often seem to run charities like personal fief-doms and without the professionalism and metrics-driven goals and measurements customary in Corporate America.

If you are exploring a start-up, spend at least a few days with your potential business partners to learn about the business, the people involved, and the way business is conducted. Are you aligned in terms of what risks you are going to take and what kind of business behavior is expected and tolerated? I once explored a start-up with a promising business model just to realize after two weeks of immersing myself in it that the people involved and the way business was performed was outside my level of comfort. I ran away as fast as I could.

Think about your choice as an option. It might or might not lead to a real deal.

11 ▪ How deeply should I stay in touch with the job market while enjoying my time off?

This is a tough one, as the answer depends on your personality, your circumstances, and the overall activity level in the job market. You have three potential approaches.

The most extreme would be to neither actively conduct nor passively be available for job conversations. This means that you make yourself unavailable, tell everybody on your social network sites, including *LinkedIn,* that you are in far away lands. You don't respond to calls from headhunters or, if you reply (as you always should), signal that you are not interested at the moment. There are benefits to this approach: first and foremost, you really take a break, a true time off, and you enjoy this period to the fullest, not being disturbed by any thoughts on jobs and job search. This might be the right way, if you are sure that you don't want to return to Corporate America or you know exactly what you want to do after your time off. By postponing conversations, you are not losing anything.

You might remember that I did recommend any trips to not exceed a few weeks. It is always good to check in and not lose contact during time off. You will have the best of both worlds by oscillating between times away (where you do not take calls and let an auto-reply do the work) and being home when you catch up and see how the economic situation might have changed. You also could check online job boards or do some research when away if you are curious about what is going on in the market. Internet cafés are everywhere. The key is never, ever to forget that your priority is to enjoy your time off. If looking at job boards or doing job research stresses you out, then don't do it. Postpone everything until the end of your trip or the end of your time off.

The worst thing you can do is taking an active job search with you. It is worse than staying home because your infrastructure will most likely be not as good, cheap, or even be available. Second, it defies the whole purpose of the gift of job loss.

12 ▪ When do I know that I should start my job search and end my time off, concluding my gift of job loss?

You know it when you are there. This sounds strange, but you will know when you have reached the point of readiness. This moment comes either gradually or suddenly like a flash, after you have seen and experienced a lot and made checkmarks behind each of the goals that you had.

You might miss work with its daily schedule, the water cooler gossip, and the security of a paycheck. You are relaxed by now and ready to give it all in the job search. You narrowed down what you want to do and can't wait to get started. You were lucky and got the "aha moment" with regard to what type of business to start. Or you were not quite done yet with all your travel plans, but the call to talk to your dream company came out of the blue and after only one round of interviews they decided to hire you on the spot.

Be flexible. Have a maximum time window for your time off, but allow for the possibility of an early ending. It is part of the fun and excitement not to know the exact end.

Your biggest challenge might be to get your discipline back. By discipline I mean focusing 100% on what is next for you, getting up early, writing job applications, networking, or doing whatever it takes to execute the next phase of your life. If you start looking for a job, you know that this will take time, probably several months. Financially, this should not be an issue, since you planned ahead and got your financial house in order and simplified your life before you took time off, right? If you have outplacement help, use it now because it will help you go toward the direction you want and enforce your discipline.

Overall, you should be well rested, full of new experiences, and happy to go back to work. You should pat yourself on the back for having gone down this path. If you took time off during a recession, you might be lucky that the economy has improved and your option to wait was worthwhile. If you explored a new location you now might be ready to move or focus your job search on this new place. Whichever of the 15 activities you enjoyed during your time off, I hope that was the right decision for you and inspired you to do the same again if the opportunity should arise.

▓ Don't worry too much—you don't have to decide and plan alone

Don't worry too much. You had a job or several before. Why wouldn't you find one again? Remember that most people regret not what they have done but what they did not do when reaching the end of their lives. Re-read the sections in *Part II* on life's time allocation and the choice you have about what "game" you play. Don't let naysayers derail you. The hardest part for you might be to figure out what you want, given the noise around you.

Friends, family, colleagues, and outplacement firms can be great resources. You should use their advice and support. There will be one thing to be aware of: you might not be getting holistic, agenda-free advice for your sole benefit only. Even the best intentioned help might suffer from lack of experience or a certain degree of selfishness.

If you need help deciding and planning your gift of job loss, you can receive independent personalized advice from me. Check out **www.thegiftofjobloss.com** for more information.

▓ ▓ ▓

EPILOGUE: THE GIFT THAT KEEPS GIVING

After my time off, I looked back at the many "ups" of the last year, the few "downs," the lessons learned, and the happiness I had enjoyed and shared with others. I realized that the gift of job loss was not coming to an end. It was a gift that would keep giving.

There were the many memories. There were souvenirs— magnets on my fridge from all corners of the world, a lovely painting from Uruguay, a rug from Peru, two bulls for my book shelf (one made of wood from Argentina, one made of steel from Peru). There were pictures that captured it all. I had visited exotic travel destinations where there might not be a decent opportunity later in life. These were experiences that nobody would be able to take away. I had met my new girlfriend in the most unlikely spot, a jungle plane, and was now deeply in love. I had created my personal little charity in Guatemala. There was a more relaxed attitude towards roadblocks in life, not least after seeing the poverty in Guatemala. I had moved and started to explore a new location in Austin, Texas. On the personal investment side, I had become a first-time, small landlord. I had spent quality time with Mom and with my best friends on unforgettable trips.

There were a few down moments during the year as well. A company had called and offered me what would have been a dream job but withdrew five days before the starting date. It was at my six months mark of time off. After the initial shock of disbelief, I turned this lemon into lemonade by extending my gift of job loss. Thus I was able to visit the most amazing ancient cities of the world.

Upon my return and in interviews I was often asked about the benefits of my time off and whether I thought it was "daring" to have done it.

I do not think that my time off was "daring," "risky," "crazy," or part of a "mid-life crisis." It might have been unusual for a former executive. This step might need some explanation, but it was not daring. It was not daring because I had taken a hard look at the trade-off of limited time for life and money when free time was given to me due to job loss. In that moment, time, which is in shorter supply than money in our life, became abundant for a limited period. I had grabbed that opportunity. In economic terms, the trade-off between work (assuming I had found a job soon) and time spent to carry out many of the 15 activities had been clearly in favor of the latter. Whether I worked from 43 years of age to 65 or from 44 to 66, it would not make a difference. Buying the insurance policy against early disease or death by pursuing certain items had been a smart and conservative move.

As expected, the option to sit out a deep recession was valuable as the economy had been improving and now offered more opportunities than before I left my last company. The economy was still far away from the old heydays, though the decision to wait instead of choosing a panic-stricken entry into a depressed labor market still seemed right. Or, if you think about opportunity costs, the opportunity costs had been close to zero, exactly as expected. Literally the day after I ended my time off, I sat in the office of two search firms discussing job opportunities.

I came back energized, full of optimism, and ready to focus 100% on business. In terms of benefits for my future professional life, the time off was meaningful as well. There was the learning of new skills, both hard and soft. Fluency in Spanish and the deepening of my experience in Latin America should serve me well professionally in the future. I had learned new things about myself, particularly how to handle uncertainty, how to relax in an economic crisis, and how to move forward when others are pessimistic. I had time to reflect upon my previous jobs, the successes and occasional issues. This reflection helped me to get more clarity about my work style, my strengths and weaknesses. Knowing myself better should come in handy in my future professional endeavors.

I had collected business ideas. I explored one of those, but a potential business partner had not shown interest. There are still more ideas being investigated and some "on the shelf." This means there might be benefits of my travel that are not known yet, that might spring into action in a few months or in a few years. In the meantime, I am growing my consulting business and working on my first teaching engagements at a university.

As an added bonus, I was even a little bit richer than a year ago. The securities markets had recovered; some optimism was back, at least sufficiently enough to make my 401K and other accounts look better. I smiled. I had not worked a single day and had spent less on all of my travel than the rent for my one-bedroom in New York would have been. My travel had been frugal, taking advantage of fare sales, optimizing frequent flyer miles, and picking non-luxurious adventure companies. I had kept my expenses manageable. Furthermore, this calculation did not factor in mentally reclassifying part of my expenses as investments. I firmly believed that some of my activities would yield higher earnings down the road.

My friends and ex-colleagues convinced me to write this book and I followed their advice. I would consider myself lucky if I managed successfully to encourage you to consider accepting the gift of job loss should it ever present itself to you.

Above all, I had realized the most important lesson: life is really amazing if you let certain things happen. One step will lead to the next, though you might not know what the next step will be.

■ ■ ■

APPENDIX A ....

Dealing with three situations you may face—
imminent job-loss; already laid off; or still "safely" employed

1 ▨ What to do when seeing job loss on the horizon

If people are honest, most would tell you that they saw "it" coming. If you are perceptive, you know when you are in danger and what a company-wide cost-cutting program can mean to you. I am not saying that you know with certainty whether you will be on the list, but very often you should be able to assess quite easily what the probabilities are for you to lose out.

Let me give you some easy signs. First of all, if you are not a top performer or not protected by the "big boss," whenever there is change coming, you are at risk. If a consulting firm is reviewing the organization, they most likely promised management at least a 20% savings on expenses. That is the magic number. Sometimes the number is higher. Unless you are a producer, generate sales directly, or happen to be the only one left to understand the legacy programming language of the mainframe computer, you are in danger. If you work in marketing, strategy, HR, or any other fair weather cost-center units like "diversity" or "innovation," you are toast. At least there is a high chance. The more you make in salary compared to peers, the higher your risk. If you are a foreign "expat" here in the US or an American abroad, your forehead has a big sign "please fire me in a recession since I cost double to triple what my peers cost." If you are the head of a unit who makes double what your next subordinate makes, be prepared to be let go and see your unit merged with another for the company to save one expensive executive. There is a similar story in the case of a merger; execution of it will take a few months, but if two units of the same function exist, this is one too many.

In all these previous examples, there was one common denominator: you did not wake up Monday morning to lose your job the same day. No, you learned about the restructuring program in April when the CEO announced results should be expected in September. For you this means getting the pink slip, if at all, around October or November. In other words, you received a warning notice. The time of uncertainty has started. People will start positioning themselves and play even more games than usual. Gossip is everywhere. You probably have experienced such a situation already. The good news is that the information about you being at risk has value as you can start preparing.

If you work in Corporate America, there is a high chance that you will receive severance payments according to your company's policy. Severance payments and severance policies are a great invention and one of your (the employee's) "best friends." Severance policies have many benefits for both your employer and for you. You need to understand them thoroughly. Please take a look at *Appendix B: A little primer on severance packages.*

What should you do in a situation when the writing is on the proverbial wall and your chance of losing your job is high? Here is the nine-step program you should consider:

STEP 1:
Decide whether you actually would like to keep your job

This is not a rhetorical question. You might have 15 years of service under your belt, be fully vested in various benefits, and are tired of the long commute. A fabulous severance package would be quite attractive to you to spend more time at home or start your dream B&B. Or the opposite, you really like the company; you have just joined, and think it would be the wrong moment to look for another job. Decide for yourself (and together with your spouse), what is your preference?

One way of making the judgment call might be to take a hard look at your role and position, the latest performance reviews, how you feel there day-in, day-out. Are your skills matched by the position you have? If you get a book like Tom Rath's *Strengthsfinder 2.0*, you might get a better self-assessment. Also, don't be shy to ask friends and former colleagues. What they tell you about yourself might be very eye-opening and helpful.

STEP 2:
Act based on your decision and options available to you

If you want to keep your job and don't find the severance option attractive or expect a better offer down the road, stay where you are, double your work effort and hope that somebody else will be asked to leave. Volunteer for more work, schmooze higher-ups, refrain from any gossip, send emails on Saturdays, just do everything all the time that demonstrates your commitment and your image as Mr. or Ms. Corporate Citizen. Should it not help you in the end, at least you tried, right?

On the other side, should you be eyeing severance, work normal business hours, strategically complain about the ineffectiveness of the ongoing cost-cutting program while you can be overheard, get a good understanding of the company's severance policy, and, if possible, tell people "as a secret" that you would be open to be "on the list." Let the invisible hand of Corporate America work its magic. If you are lucky, you will get your wish.

STEP 3:
Try to keep your fear in check

It is just a probability that you may lose your job, not a certainty. It is a bit like waiting for a medical test when waiting is worse than the actual result. Think about the many people who were better off after lay-off, and don't focus on the horror stories you read in the press. Work on the next steps outlined below.

STEP 4:
Get clarity on the activities you would pursue after losing your job

Start dreaming a bit. Take a look at the 15 activities and think which ones might appeal to you. You might even start doing some research on a country you would like to visit or inquire about a certain charity. If you keep your job after all, you learned something new. You might still go to that country at a later time or help the charity otherwise. But for now, imagine what you would do. I would hope that this exercise will also help you stay calm, because you realize that you have a "Plan B."

STEP 5:
Stay healthy and improve your health

Going to the gym or doing other sports and exercises is good for you physically and psychologically. It makes you feel better about yourself and reduces stress. It is no coincidence that this is also a no-regret activity to do (Activity #3). You might not have that much time at this point, but try making an effort. Finally think about health care. If you have company health care and notwithstanding the changing landscape of health insurance, now might be a good time to inquire about an individual health policy as often this is a smarter choice than taking COBRA (if offered).

STEP 6:
Bring your life up to date and simplify it for the future

This is a no-regret move (Activity #4) for time after job loss. Independent of your future employment status, reducing clutter in your life is always beneficial. It is even more beneficial when faced with a potential job loss. You have less to worry about, financially and otherwise. Cancel old subscriptions, concentrate your time on charities that really matter, and check out the worth of your home or apartment. Throw 30% of unneeded stuff away, at least. Getting rid of old papers, cleaning out the garage, and selling the old lamp on *eBay* will make you feel good. And if you do it now, you will have more time after your job loss and can go right into a nice vacation. This might also be a good moment to consider selling your rental property, if you have one, in case it caused you more grief than income.

STEP 7:
Get your financial house in order

This gives you an early start for this no-regret move (Activity #5). It helps you determine what would be financially feasible after job loss. How large would severance be? Add everything up—the notification period salary, the severance based on the formula in place, and any immediate vesting of restricted stocks and options. Add up all your savings. How much do you have?

Exercise any stock options you have at the company (if they are worth something). Don't bet the farm on exotic investments anymore. Pay back credit card debt, refinance your mortgage, and take a hard look at your spending patterns. Don't engage in any consumer purchases on credit, in particular no installment plans that make you pay back over years. What expenses can be reduced now? What could be reduced after job loss?

The earlier you get a grip on your finances and understand the ramifications of a job loss, the better prepared you will be. And the more freedom you will have to pursue the various alternatives to immediate job search instead of going right at it. Use a financial and/or tax advisor to plan how to get the most out of expected job loss, if you need help, or look for some book resources in *Appendix C*.

Finally, prepare your family, partner, etc. Don't hide, don't make it a surprise. Start reducing expenses gradually. Involve everybody in the family. Spending time with kids in a public park can be quite as much fun as going on an expensive roller coaster or to a theme park.

STEP 8:
Try to understand the timeline in your company

When will decisions be made and announced? Is there a rush to beat the year-end and get people out before? Are you protected by mandatory notification rules of your state, such as 60 days, 90 days? Estimate the timeline and listen to the rumors. If you have a good connection to HR or your boss, you might get some unofficial ranges.

STEP 9:
Relax

You did everything you potentially could do. You are well pre-pared for either scenario (job loss vs. continued employment). You are most likely better prepared than anybody around you. Realize that certain things are outside your control. You can prepare to a certain point, after which you have to sit back, relax, and wait. This is such a situation.

2 ▪ What to do after just being let go?

You bought this book after just being escorted out or handing in your corporate badge. Maybe you were let go yesterday, a few weeks ago, or even a few months ago. You might have already started looking for a new job and are the first few weeks into it.

Here are my four recommendations for you:

RECOMMENDATION 1:
Leave the past behind

The biggest mistake you can make is living in the past. Unless you have to or they are true friends of yours, stop talking to old colleagues. Your old company is of no concern to you anymore. Same goes for spending time with other laid-off people from the same company. Yes, you might let out some steam, but if done too much, it prevents you from moving on. It will neither help you find a new job nor regain your optimism.

Don't hide in your basement and avoid telling people about your situation. Don't dress up in the morning to impress the neighbors. Instead walk over, let them know that you are now starting a new phase in your life, but first you are going to take a long-needed vacation.

RECOMMENDATION 2:
Acknowledge that this new situation takes some adjustment

You can expect to feel a bit disoriented after not going to work anymore. A friend of mine compares the situation to "bumping into trees" until you find your bearings. This is one of the reasons that "doing nothing" for a while after job loss is crucial (Activity #1); it helps you find that adjustment. The feeling of being disoriented is stronger, the shorter the time has been between learning about your job loss and the time it actually happened.

RECOMMENDATION 3:
Implement the 7 no-regret activities faster the longer you have already been out of work

Unless you have done so already, take a fun trip, one of the first activities when losing a job (Activity #2). You need a break, no matter how tough you think you are. Urgently do what I recommended with regard to staying healthy (Activity #3), simplifying your life (Activity #4), and getting your finances in order (Activity #5); you now just have to do it faster to make up for time.

RECOMMENDATION 4:

Assess the job market situation and calculate how much time you would need for any optional activities important to you

It is not too late to follow through with some activities from the list of the 8 optional activities, in particular if you would not be losing much.

For example, if you only have negative responses to your job search so far, this might be the right time to step back and refrain from actively looking for a job for a while. You might be able to put outplacement services on hold and interrupt your search.

Take a look at any seasonality of your job market (e.g., spring and fall as the main hiring seasons). Calculate how long a job search would take based on your location, economy, and seniority. If the economy is bad and you are already in May without a job offer, you should seriously consider taking June to August off from your search. The option to wait might be in your favor while you can pursue items from your "bucket list." You could focus on learning something new (Activity #9), enjoy a once-in-a-lifetime trip (Activity #6), explore charity work as a career option (Activity #15), or find the true "you" (Activity #13). Then you will come back in September, rested and re-energized to move on.

If your job loss happens in a deep recession, the doors in your town or industry might be closed for job seekers for a long time. It could be time to explore alternatives like a different location (Activity #11), a new career (Activity #15), or going back to school (Activity #8).

3 ▪ "Safely" employed—preparing for job loss years ahead

Congratulations to you! While many of your peers and friends might be without a job in these challenging times, you are employed and hopefully enjoy what you do. Congratulations also for buying this book. You understand that no matter how safe you feel right now or how well your career is going, things could change very suddenly. Feeling safe does not mean you *are* safe. In fact, my personal experience is as follows: things are never as bad as they look and never as good as they look. If you have trouble with your boss and everything looks desperate, your boss might leave the company and everything takes a turn for the better. When you are happily cruising along, counting your stock options and looking forward to the next promotion, your company announces a surprising loss, your shares tank, and the consultants are called in to lower costs by 20%. Never be too smug, never be too down. Things seldom are what they appear and never, ever stay the same.

Many people will at least once in their lifetime lose employment involuntarily—independent of the level of hierarchy, tenure, or identification with and commitment to the company.

By reading this book, you are willing to look ahead and spare some thoughts on the future for yourself or somebody else close to you. Maybe you bought this book for a friend facing job loss but not before reading it yourself first! Alternatively, you may just want to get some ideas and start dreaming about time off. Either way, you are making the right move.

If you are gainfully employed and feel safe for now, my advice to you consists of four pillars:

PILLAR 1:
Save, save, save

The best time to save is when you are fully employed. You get your regular paycheck. Some parts of the pay you receive are inside, some outside your control (like stock options). I would recommend you save up to one full annual salary (after taxes) as your emergency budget. This is higher than many financial advisers recommend, but trust me, having a year of money in the bank, stashed in safe CDs or savings accounts, feels pretty good. It is a great insurance policy and, most of all, gives you a certain independence and peace of mind. If your salary exceeds your living costs significantly, it would be fine to save up to 12 months of monthly living costs, whatever this might be in terms of salary.

If you receive severance as well, your money will stretch easily up to 15 or even 18 months, not counting unemployment benefits you might be getting. You should think in terms of how long money would last to determine how much to save. Some costs might go down dramatically like commuting costs. On the other side, extra money would be a fantastic cushion to do many of the 15 activities outlined earlier. Six months of savings might be plenty, if you get six months of severance, but twelve months are always better. The less you are dependent on the job, the better off you will be mentally and the more likely you will not find yourself in panic mode. Very calmly you can take the advice of this book and enjoy your post-employment status.

PILLAR 2:
Create your "bucket list"

The second task for you should be creating your "bucket list." Don't forget to involve your spouse. Talk about your unfulfilled dreams, and discuss what the two of you would do if one or both of you were being laid off. Would you stay put, take a dream vacation, quit to start something new together, move? The 15 potential activities should serve as a guide. Write the results down on paper and re-visit them from time to time. It might all be far off now, but having the little sheet of paper handy to pull out if the ax falls, can be very helpful.

PILLAR 3:
Think ahead about in which circumstances you would take severance or even leave on your own

If you are financially stable or even protected by law or internal company policies against lay-off, you might want to ask yourself the tougher question:

"Since I will never be given the gift of job loss by my company, at what point, at what age should I take the initiative, if any, to leave on my own? At what point does the trade-off of money and time to travel or start something new tilt in favor of the latter, even if I am not given money by the company to leave?"

Some of my friends pointed out that if you take the message of this book seriously, why wait to be fired? You might choose to call the shots and make the choice alone, not waiting for somebody else to decide for you. They have a point, although it is tough enough for people to accept the benefits of job loss when handed to them. It is even more difficult for most to pull the trigger themselves.

PILLAR 4:
Consider which parts of your "bucket list" you can start implementing while being employed

The older you are, the less time is left to fulfill your dreams that you have not realized yet. You also have a higher chance of getting sick or even dying, as we outlined earlier in this book. Hence, once you have your "bucket list," you might want to see what you can do while being employed. Maybe you go on shorter trips, use the sabbatical policy of your company to take some time off for a dream vacation, shift your work-life balance to engage with a charity, or reject internal new tasks or new jobs that are too taxing on your health. Whatever you can realize from your "bucket list" or might help you live longer, do it. Your company might also offer part-time flexibility or the chance to work remotely from home. This would also allow you to do more things outside work that are important to you. Free time for you might be more valuable at your age or point in your life than the associated reduction in paycheck.

In summary, enjoy your career to the fullest, save, and don't forget to live life. Have your "bucket list" and rough ideas of which of the 15 activities you would pursue, if fired, at hand! Like the fire emergency training at your workplace when they show you where the staircase is to leave the building, having money saved and your plan ready are your ticket to happiness when thrown off the corporate bus.

■ ■ ■

APPENDIX B...

A little primer on severance packages

Severance policies are beneficial for both you and the employer. They are a true benefit for you, one of the best left in Corporate America.

First of all, having a standardized severance policy in place reduces transaction costs. There is no need for individual bargaining and involving employment lawyers.

Second, a good severance policy is a great antidote to the "employment at will" character of your employment, putting a floor on your "loss" when losing your job, unless you are fired "for cause," in which case you will go empty handed. Severance policies, if transparent, allow you to assess pretty well in advance what you will get in case of involuntary job loss. The official policies might even get better in special situations like a merger. I strongly recommend you check out a company's severance policy before joining. Most large companies are transparent about these policies. I think it is only fair for you to know what happens after you walk into their door, and a few days later your unit is closed down. If a company does not reveal its policy to you, ask around about what the policy currently is or how the company acted in the past. In case of doubt, do not join a company that does not have a good severance policy. These policies are more valuable than other perks like gym memberships or a few thousand dollars more in annual salary. Severance policies are your insurance. This is probably the only real perk left when working for a large corporation outside Cadillac health plans or generous option grants, if you are senior enough to get these benefits.

Severance policies have some interesting economics. There is usually a minimum benefit you get from day one on your job, and then this benefit rises with your tenure at the firm, but levels off at a maximum that you can get. The level of severance depends on your seniority as well. A Vice President will mostly get both longer severance (e.g., six months) and additional benefits (e.g., outplacement service) than a lower level employee (e.g., six weeks, no outplacement).

It is usually quite lucrative to get dismissed right after starting your job if you consider how much money you receive (earnings plus severance) for just a short time at work. As mentioned, the absolute benefits increase with tenure, but it is fairly common for them to level off. Many large companies—less so with smaller companies—have something like the following in place: Minimum severance, say, three months of salary, then two weeks for each year served, maxing out at one year total. In other words, it makes a difference whether you have worked one day (three months severance), one year and one day (three months + two weeks severance), or 19 years (three months plus 19 x 2 weeks severance = about 52 weeks or one year). Thereafter (i.e., 20+ years in our example), additional time does not add to your severance. Also, when there is severance, it is fairly common that any stock award vests immediately, and many corporations let you vest unvested company contributions to retirement accounts.

One of the biggest benefits of severance policies to employers is that you only receive severance after you sign that you are not going to sue for wrongful dismissal. The company does not need to spend money on lawyers or defend itself in court because you feel that you got dismissed for being a woman, a minority, gay, or unlawfully dismissed for whatever reason. This makes the calculation of dismissals easy and predictable...for both sides.

Instead of big cost-cutting programs mentioned earlier, sometimes cost reduction happens in a less obvious way, or on a much smaller level and with less noise. A company might decide to cut across the board 5% and leave it up to each manager to find a way, or better, to determine who should leave the company. In other words, there is some leeway in who is being affected and the timing of the job loss. Maybe the budget is cut in one area and only affects one or two people out of 20. These are the situations where severance payments can become *your* best friend, your personal "put option." It is not uncommon for companies to look for volunteers to take severance, officially or without announcement. Now might be the time for you to talk in confidence to your boss or HR representative. If you are lucky, you might get a better deal than the standard severance policy. Indicate that you would be open to leave, but not before a certain day or only in combination with a consulting contract. The severance might be as generous as winning the lottery—several months of salary, some bonus, vesting of the stock you fear might tank anyhow, health care benefits, etc.

Needless to say, if you want to keep your job and don't find the severance option attractive at this point or expect a better offer down the road, you can stay where you are, double your work effort and hope that somebody else will be asked to leave. You have no guarantee, but at least you tried.

It is also important to note that there could be several rounds of lay-offs. Sometimes companies announce multiple rounds of lay-offs in advance. Even if there is no formal announcement for multiple rounds, you usually have a good feel for whether there will be "more rounds to come." Severance packages are not stable, though. They are not written in stone like the Ten Commandments once were. It is not uncommon to see a company reduce the severance benefits from lay-off round to lay-off round. There can be several potential reasons for that. Sometimes, the company just does not have the money anymore. Think of a steel mill that reduces its workforce just to survive. The first people that leave still get some compensation, the rest.....good luck. Or it is done by design—a company might want to induce people to leave early, in particular the more expensive older ones on solid pension plans, or expensive higher ups. By offering a generous policy upfront, employees will be confronted with the following choice: accept now and leave with a generous package but be unemployed earlier, or hold out, keep the job for now, but maybe get a worse package later...the devil you know vs. the devil you don't know. While it is difficult to give you a general recommendation, my bias would be to get out fast. Pocket the money while it is there for you. Leave with the satisfaction that you had at least some say in your own termination. Don't waste any more time in a company where your time is limited. Be an optimist. Avoid the backstabbing and depressive atmosphere in a company whose employees know that more cuts are to come. Start enjoying the various activities of the gift of job loss.

▩ ▩ ▩

APPENDIX C..
Selected literature

We touched upon many topics in the main parts of the book. I would expect that there are some topics that you would like to know more about. Instead of just dumping a list of resources on you, I take a different approach. For each major topic I will point you to the best books I could find and describe what makes them worthwhile reading. This approach should be time efficient for you. It relieves you of the burden of selecting among a sometimes agonizing choice of similar reading material.

The Gift of Job Loss should just be the starting point for your journey. My book is not intended to be a tactical book duplicating information that can be found elsewhere. That is where this section should come in handy for you.

I have read all the books that I selected for you below. The opinion regarding what makes them useful is clearly my own. Many books are good on many aspects and could appear in several categories. For example, Tim Ferriss' *The 4-Hour Workweek* is probably the most "jack-of-all-trade" books as it offers ideas and resources on many fronts, from travel to finding alternatives to Corporate America.

Most authors update and revise their books after a while. When you buy anything from my selection, make sure you get the latest version.

Here are the categories of my literature recommendations:

1. Losing your job—how to cope with it and how to make the most of it
2. Philosophical musings on the subject and importance of "time" in our life
3. Your time off—financial preparation and planning
4. Travel—all the basic resources you will ever need
5. The importance of location—how to select a city in which to work and live
6. Finding your true "calling" and profession
7. Exploring career alternatives to Corporate America

You will find the publisher details in the *Bibliography* at the end of the book.

1 ▪ Losing your job—how to cope with it and how to make the most of it

There are four books that should warrant your attention.

First, I recommend famous management guru Harvey Mackay's *We Got Fired!* for inspiration. You learn how even the most famous people got fired at least once in their lifetime. You read what they did and what you can learn from their experience. Mackay has peppered the book with many lessons about how you can get back onto your feet quickly. It is a great read.

Thank You for Firing Me! is based on Kitty Martini's and Candice Reed's research on people who were let go. It is a very practical guide on what to do and what to explore, including the usual alternatives to Corporate America. It addresses the topic of drifting after job loss, gives great advice like avoiding "rebound" work, and makes a good effort at proposing industries and trends of the future that could be out there for you (e.g., green industries, jobs targeting boomers). The book also has an extensive listing of resources helpful for the unemployed.

The next two books are personal accounts of what people did with their life after job loss. If you like reading emotional, though uplifting personal stories, Lee Kravitz's ...*unfinished business*...and Dominique Browning's *Slow Love* will be your cup of tea.

Kravitz used his unemployment to catch up with life in a very special way. He addressed "wrongs" he did in the past, finished things he started, and in general used one year off "trying to do the right things." In other words, he used his time strategically for things important to him, things that he had forgotten about and had not been able to do during employment.

Browning's story of using her time of unemployment is less focused on certain goals. Her account is about the personal ups and downs, the discovery of the beauty of life after her center of life—a big job—was history. She gives emotional accounts of moving out of her family house and other personal stories. Her history might interest you if you define your life mainly by your work and wonder what you would do if you lose this anchor. Browning openly shares her feelings about the dramatic change of being an important businesswoman for years, and then suddenly waking up as somebody looking for meaning outside work.

2 ▪ **Philosophic musings on the subject and importance of "time" in our lives**

The meaning of time, our life's time, the meaning of death—all these related topics have been on the human mind for thousands of years. I have come across two phenomenal books that address the issue of "time" for us worker bees very nicely.

One of the tenets of *The Gift of Job Loss* is that our life is finite and you don't know how long you have left on earth. That is why when you lose your job, you should seriously consider using time, your resource in short supply, strategically. If you need more theoretical, philosophical, or inspirational support for my thesis, go straight to *Time and the Art of Living*, written by Robert Grudin, an English professor. He has composed a marvelous book. Grudin's book contains hundreds of little paragraphs full of musings and thoughts on time; what time means for us and what it *should* mean for us. He analyzes time from various angles: how time relates to love, politics, age, morality and everything else important in our lives. He shows us how we are deceived by our subjective perception of time and held hostage by it. This book is so rich and thought provoking, you have to read it slowly. You need to take breaks to contemplate its meaning. Take a pen and mark the important messages for you, of which there will be many.

The second book along similar lines, though with easier prose, is Jean-Louis Servan-Schreiber's *The Art of Time*. He looks straight at our deficits when it comes to managing our time. Addressing the many culprits for our lack of time, his European perspective should be a great eye opener for any of you who are held hostage to the work ethic and education that places work life above everything else. He addresses issues like couples being too stressed for having sex anymore and how our modern life is going against what defines us as human beings. Servan-Schreiber makes you think about your priorities in life. That means the priorities of how you spend time. He also gives concrete advice on how to get some of your time back by re-setting priorities. Whether you read Grudin's or this book first, it does not matter—but read them both.

3 ▪ Your time off—financial preparation and planning

There are a few authors who have done an excellent job in putting "time off" into a step-by-step action plan. Their kind of detailed planning might not be for everyone. If you like some hand-holding or are afraid that money might run out, these books are for you. All of them offer some perspective on the benefits and fears of taking a sabbatical. They are written by no-nonsense financial planners and HR people, which should comfort anybody from Corporate America.

In *Power Sabbatical*, Robert Levine offers a project plan approach to taking a sabbatical. From goal setting to financial planning to practical arrangements, it is all there. My recommendation for you is to get familiar with Chapters 3, *Sizing it up* and 5, *Paying for it*. They are little treasures of checklists that might guide your own planning. Other chapters are a good read as well (for example his thoughts on how to handle objections in Chapter 10). Just be aware that some recommendations might not apply to you because his book targets mainly people who return to their previous job. If there is only one "sabbatical book" you buy, get this one.

My other favorite is *Escape 101*. It deals with the mental roadblocks you face, be it financial or family/children, and how to overcome them. It also talks at length about the benefits of taking time off and what it takes to make this period of your life successful. I like that the book is conservative when it comes to planning, both financial and otherwise. The book deals at length with arguments for sabbaticals and identifies them correctly as an investment in your future. It explains the many benefits of them, and deals with fears and anxiety. The authors, Dan Clements and Tara Gignac, provide good thoughts on the time after your time off as well. Overall, *Escape 101* is a solid book that makes preparation for your potential time off much easier.

There are two more books. They are a bit dated, but still good reads. Like all "sabbatical books," they target people who have a job and still need to negotiate time off from work; therefore many pages are devoted to dealing with your company. This is obviously no concern for you in the case of lay-off. Nevertheless, both books offer good stimulating thoughts, in particular for those of you who have a hard time thinking that life can be worthwhile if you don't work for a few months. Lisa Angowski Rogak's *Time Off from Work* is at its best in Chapter 2 when she discusses how a sabbatical might affect your career. She deals with the many myths and truths about sabbaticals. I also like her approach to naysayers (Chapter 7), something that should apply in your situation as well. *Six Months Off* by Hope Dlugozima, James Scott, and David Sharp, has many of the same benefits as Rogak's book. It is great on motivation and dealing with potential roadblocks. It also has a few inspiring case studies. I like that it briefly deals with sabbaticals after lay-off, though

I don't agree with the term "forced sabbatical." There should be nothing forced about taking time off. Large parts of the book provide names of organizations that can help with spiritual or charity sabbaticals.

A final light read is Nancy-Whitney Reiter's *Unplugged*. Reiter left Corporate America to travel, and the book deals with all aspects of taking a sabbatical. She describes at length the benefits of taking time off and travel. There are many inspiring case studies. While not as deep as other books on resources or planning, she gives good common-sense advice. I like her recommendation that some part of any sabbatical time should be undertaken alone.

4 ▪ Travel—all the basic resources you will ever need

PREPARATION AND PLANNING

When it comes to travel resources, there is no shortage both on the Internet and in the form of books. There are travel booking sites like *www.travelocity.com* or *www.orbitz.com*, and travel advisory sites like *www.tripadvisor.com*, Hotels, airlines, and travel magazines have their own websites. The choice can be overwhelming. Before you book your travel and go, you want to think about the "what" and the "where," the "how long" and "how." You want to maximize the benefits of your time off, and you want to focus on what makes you the most happy.

Buying books online is fine but nothing beats being in a *Barnes & Noble*, *Borders*, or your local bookstore and wandering around in the travel section. Travelogues, travel guides, maps—the world is your oyster. Generally speaking, my favorite travel guides are *Rough Guides* and *Fodor's*, as they cover all kinds of travel and are practical, while giving great detail on cultural background.

There are three books that are the best of the breed when it comes to thinking and planning for global, meaningful, or long-time travel. They all have their own websites with updated resources. These are the only books you will ever need when it comes to your travel apart from travel guides for your destinations.

The "bible," or rather the dictionary of travel sabbaticals is a British book, called *Gap Years for Grown Ups*. Susan Griffith's well-rounded mix of travel ideas, inspiration, advice, travel resources, and case studies should be beneficial to you, in particular if your travel experience is limited. Griffith calls her book "the most comprehensive, practical guide to taking a career break," and at least with regard to travel and the kind of travel (adventure, charity/volunteering, etc.), she is right. The book contains some advertisements by third parties, but they actually enhance the book. The book seems to be updated frequently. The slightly European perspective is refreshing because many travel resources listed are not the ones you might find in American books. Since travel is a big and very professionally organized industry in Europe, her resource lists should be very valuable to you.

Vagabonding—An Uncommon Guide to the Art of Long-term World Travel is much better than the title may suggest. Forget about his marketing word "vagabonding" and what it potentially means. The fact is that Rolf Potts deals with all potential issues of long-term travel. Potts lists tremendous resources, and offers down-to-earth advice through inspiring case studies. He asks the right questions about what you should do with your life. I just loved this book, in particular its slightly philosophical touch enhanced by famous quotes while firmly being grounded in reality. He deals with how to behave when traveling, how to get the most out of it, and how to preserve the benefits when you return. His "tip sheets" on online and other resources are focused, helpful, and with a reason given why he selected them for you. I also liked his lists of spiritual travel readings and his tips for seniors and families.

The last book on this mandatory list is Timothy Ferriss' *The 4-Hour Workweek*. Ferris coined the term "mini-retirements," essentially time off between jobs. His book also deals with many issues, alternatives to Corporate America, how to outsource time-consuming tasks to third parties, how to optimize your work life when employed, and how to find income on the Internet. His own story includes a lot of travel, and that's why his philosophy on travel and the resources he provides are first-class. He is inspirational. His approach to travel and time off makes this bestseller a great read. But, similar to *Vagabonding*, don't take the marketing-driven title of this book too seriously. Ferriss most likely works more than four hours a week. Focus on the content, the inspirational case studies, his clear analysis, and the abundance of resources for you to explore. His list of resources is not as broad and deep as Potts and there is some natural overlap between the two; together these two books are an unbeatable combo.

TRAVEL FOR INVESTING AND TRAVEL WITH KIDS

I mentioned Gary Hoover in the main section and his views that entrepreneurs should travel. You also know that travel opens your horizons culturally and you can pick up ideas that you can use in Corporate America or otherwise. Travel is also important if you want to invest globally or think about relocating.

With regard to travel and investing, I would like to point you to two classics. I am talking about the travelogues of two famous investors and fund managers, Mark Mobius and Jim Rogers. They are still around and you can see them on the typical business TV channels. For inspiration, read Mark Mobius' *Passport to Profits* in which he describes his visits to companies and countries in emerging markets; his investment philosophy is as important today as it was when he wrote the book over a decade ago. He was one of the pioneers in investing in these developing countries. My all-time favorite is Jim Rogers' bestseller *Investment Biker*, about his trip around the world on a motorcycle. His cross-over travel/investment book has never been copied. You can learn from his observations in the countries he traveled to—what the signs of decline are, and what signs indicate a change for the better.

The books listed earlier in "Your time off—financial preparation and planning" include a few tips and tricks on how to do a sabbatical with kids. It might be even more interesting for you to read real stories of families who took their kids, from toddlers to teens, and traveled the world. I point you to two travelogues that give vivid accounts of this feast. It takes some organization, home schooling, and certain preparation in case you want to travel for a long time (what I usually don't recommend). Reading the stories of these parents could be an eye opener for you not to dismiss the idea of time off after job loss when kids are in the picture.

My favorite is *One Year Off—Leaving It All Behind for a Round-the-World Journey with Our Children*. David Elliott Cohen, a New York Times bestselling author, describes how he, his wife and three kids of various ages planned, traveled, and returned after a year away. Contrary to many boring travelogues, this one is well-written and sometimes funny. It gives you insights into the ups and downs, including the emotions of the family. It is a great motivational read for families with kids.

I also like *World Trek—A Family Odyssey* by Russell and Carla Fisher. They are from a small Texas town and took their children on an unforgettable trip. If you like detailed travelogues, this one is for you. One added bonus of this book is its Appendix A. Fisher gives detailed information how the family planned and budgeted for their trip. This real life example might be a good complement to the books listed above under "Your time off—financial preparation and planning."

5 ▪ The importance of location—how to select a city to work and live

There is only one book to read: Richard Florida's *Who's Your City?* His analysis of how cities influence our success in career, mating, and happiness is second to none. This book should help you make better decisions regarding the location you pick to live. Choosing the right city for you will determine your well-being more than you might have thought. Travel allows you to test alternative places to live. *Who's Your City?* should be mandatory reading for you whether your search for a new location involves the US (the focus of Florida's book) or an international destination.

6 ▪ Finding your true "calling" and profession

If there is one field of self-help literature that has exploded over the last years, it is everything related to finding happiness and your "calling," your purpose in life. The number of books out there is staggering. After you get inspired by Paulo Coelho's *The Alchemist*, you need to find your own "calling." This comes down to what your passion is, what you would like to do, and what you are able to do. In other words, you have to have both the "will" and the "skill." In order to get there, it is useful to look at the way you like to work (alone vs. group), how you think (logically vs. empathically), how you communicate (extrovert vs. introvert), and how you place along dozens of other personal and work-style dimensions. Many self-tests are on the market. They allow you to figure out where you stand and what you do best. Rightly, some also target broader questions like your mission in life and what you want to achieve to be remembered.

Over the years I have come across many self-help career books. Let me share with you the three books that impressed me the most. You might want to ultimately pick the one you feel the most comfortable with, be it from my list or not. Each of the self-help books asks you to do some work. Instead of picking several books, just pick the one or at most two that you feel are best for you.

My first suggested book is *The Big Game* by Scott MacMillan. It is a workbook that allows you to build the strong personal foundation necessary for living life on your own terms. The book talks about ten strategies and really covers all aspects of life. It is a book about your life strategy, including your career. Building blocks of MacMillan's thinking are mastering self-discipline, personal integrity, getting satisfaction, and ultimately achievement. The book is about personal development and very thought provoking.

The second book is focused on your business strengths and discovering your natural talents. It is aptly named *Strengthsfinder 2.0*. It provides you with the many different aspects of your strong suits, helps you uncover them, and use them to guide your life from there. The best part of the book is one important though simple message: put energy in leveraging and improving your strengths. Too many of us are trained to work on our weaknesses, usually a futile undertaking. Better we learn and expand on what we are best at. *Strengthsfinder 2.0* is a great self-discovery tool related to the workplace. The book will not tell you what your next job should be, but it helps you lay the foundation.

To narrow down your career options, go to *Discovering Your Career in Business* by Timothy Butler and James Waldroop. This career counseling guide comes with sophisticated self-assessment tools. I know people who used this book successfully. The book forces you to think about the choices you make. It provides inspiring case studies, and through a self-test ultimately confirms or leads to your ideal career profile and associated jobs you might seek. The authors also tackle "siren songs," people and factors in our lives that might steer us away from our best course.

7 ▪ Exploring career alternatives to Corporate America

Four books caught my attention. They should all be on your book shelf if you are seriously considering leaving Corporate America. They should help you make a strategic decision.

Caught Between a Dream and a Job by Delatorro McNeal II is a great start to explore where you stand in your current job vs. where you want to go. McNeal's book goes deep. He shows you how to get to the point of living with a purpose and with happiness.

The book tries to help you bridge your current situation with your business dream. The book allows for much soul-searching. McNeal has a religious touch, though he is non-intrusive. The book is very practical, has nice "to-do" summaries, and many self-tests. It connects well with the reader and avoids the loftiness of many other self-help books. I love the part in which McNeal makes you think about the ten items that should be on your tombstone, thereby forcing you to think about purpose in your life. If you are still employed or are about to be let go, this book makes for a great read to help you chart the right course.

The next three books make for easy reading, yet are utterly helpful. They provide inspiration with dozens of case studies, help you think through the pros and cons of alternatives to Corporate America, and provide ample resources for you to explore.

These books are:

- *I Don't Know What I Want, but I Know It's Not This* by Julie Jansen
- *Escape the Mid-Career Doldrums* by Marcia Worthing and Charles Buck, and lastly
- *Escape from Corporate America*—A practical guide to creating the career of your dreams by Pamela Skillings

All of them can serve as signposts for your journey. You should have them on your desk.

▦ ▦ ▦

BIBLIOGRAPHY

Books

Browning, Dominique. *Slow Love: How I Lost My Job, Put on My Pajamas and Found Happiness.* New York: Atlas & Co., 2010.

Butler, Timothy, PhD and Waldroop, James, PhD. *Discovering Your Career in Business.* Reading: Perseus Books, 1997.

Clements, Dan and Gignac, Tara, ND. *Escape 101—Sabbaticals Made Simple—The Four Secrets to Taking a Career Break without Losing Your Money or Your Mind.* Brainranch, 2007.

Coelho, Paulo. *The Alchemist.* New York: HarperCollins, 2006.

Cohen, David Elliot. *One Year Off—Leaving It All Behind for a Round-the-World Journey with our Children.* San Francisco: Traveler Tales', Inc, 2001.

Dlugozima, Hope, Scott, James, and Sharp, David. *Six Months Off—How to Plan, Negotiate, and Take the Break You Need without Burning Bridges or Going Broke.* New York: An Owl book, 1996.

Fisher, Russell and Carla. *World Trek—A Family Odyssey.* Highland City: Rainbow Books, Inc., 2007.

Ferriss, Timothy. *The 4-Hour Workweek: Escape 9-5, Live Anywhere, and Join the New Rich.* New York: Crown Publishers, 2007.

Florida, Richard. *Who's Your City?—How the Creative Economy Is Making Where to Live the Most Important Decision of Your Life.* New York: Basic Books, 2008.

Griffith, Susan. *Gap Years for Grown Ups, because Gap Years are Wasted on the Young.* Richmond: Crimson Publishing, 2008.

Grudin, Robert. *Time and the Art of Living*. New York: Ticknor & Fields, 1982.

Jansen, Julie. *I Don't Know What I Want, but I Know It's Not This— A Step-by-Step Guide to Finding Gratifying Work*. New York; Penguin, 2010.

Kravitz, Lee. *...unfinished business...One Man's Extraordinary Year of Trying to Do the Right Things*. New York: Bloomsbury, 2010.

Levine, Robert. *Power Sabbatical—The Break that Makes a Difference*. Findhorn: Findhorn Press, 2007.

Mackay, Harvey. *We Got Fired!....And It's the Best Thing that Ever Happened to Us* (New York: Ballantine Books, 2004)

MacMillan, Scott. *The Big Game—10 Strategies for Winning at Life*. St. Paul: Llewellyn Publications, 2003.

Martini, Kitty and Reed, Candice. *Thank You for Firing Me! How to Catch the Next Wave of Success after You Lose Your Job*. New York/London: Sterling, 2010.

McNeal II, Delatorro. *Caught Between a Dream and a Job—How to Leave the 9-5 Behind and Step into the Life You've Always Wanted*. Lake Mary: Excel Books, 2008.

Mobius, Mark, with Fenichell, Stephen. *Passport to Profits—Why the Next Investment Windfalls Will Be Found Abroad—and How to Grab Your Share*. New York: Warner Books, 1999.

Potts, Rolf. *Vagabonding—An Uncommon Guide to the Art of Long-Term World Travel*. New York: Villard, 2003.

Rath, Tom. *Strengthsfinder 2.0*. New York: Gallup Press, 2007.

Rock, Lisa Angowski. *Time Off from Work—Using Sabbaticals to Enhance Your Life while Keeping Your Career on Track*. New York: John Wiley & Sons, Inc., 1994.

Rogers, Jim. *Investment Biker—Around the World with Jim Rogers*. New York: Random House Trade Paperbacks, 2003.

Servan-Schreiber, Jean-Louis. *The Art of Time—Gain New Mastery over Your Life and the Power to Live Your Time Instead of Simply Spending It*. New York: Marlowe & Company, 2000.

Skillings, Pamela. *Escape from Corporate America—A Practical Guide to Creating the Career of Your Dreams*. New York: Ballantine Books, 2008.

Various authors. *The Wall Street Journal Guidebooks*.

Whitney-Reiter, Nancy. *Unplugged—How to Disconnect from the Rat Race, Have an Existential Crisis, and Find Meaning and Fulfillment*. Boulder: Sentient Publications, 2008.

Worthing, Marcia L. and Buck, Charles A. *Escape the Mid-Career Doldrums—What to Do Next when You're Bored, Burned Out, Retired, or Fired*. Hoboken: John Wiley & Sons, Inc., 2008.

Articles

"Lifelong Learners Make the Best Entrepreneurs: Here's How," *Austin Business Journal*, May 29-June 3, 2010

"Asia Gains, US Drops in Competitiveness," *Bloomberg Business Week*, May 19, 2010

"Need a Job? Look to Asia as Hiring Set to Rise," *CNBC.com*, July 2, 2010

"The Charms of Canada," and "The Goldilocks Recovery," *The Economist*, May 8, 2010

"Can Money Set You Free?," *Financial Times*, January 30/31, 2010

"Improving Economy Starts to Turn Tide for US Labor Market," *Financial Times*, May 18, 2010

"Wake-up Call? It's About Time, Mrs. Moneypenny," *Financial Times*, June 19/20, 2010

"Taking a Year Off without Ruining Your Career," *Forbes*, Dec 9, 2007

"Downshift," *Forbes*, April 26, 2010

"Investigate Before You Expatriate," Investment Guide Retirement, *Forbes*, June 28, 2010

"Weathering a Long Job Search," *Money*, April 2010

"The Crisis is (Mostly) Over, Now What?" and "The Best Advice Now, and Ever—The New Path, 31 Ways to Improve Your Finances," *Money*, April 2010

"5 Secrets of Highly Successful Career Changers," *Money*, June 2010

"Spend Smarter, Be Happier," *Money*, June 2010

"The Next Best Career Move: Actually Moving," *Wall Street Journal*, April 13, 2010

"A Lament for the Class of 2010," *Wall Street Journal*, May 15-16, 2010

"What Will Be the Hot Jobs of 2018," *Wall Street Journal*, May 26, 2010

"Cost-cutting Detroit Will Close 77 Parks," *Wall Street Journal*, June 25, 2010

"How to Get Your Groove Back," *Wall Street Journal*, July 6, 2010

ACKNOWLEDGMENTS

My deepest thanks go to my friends who gave me candid feedback on the first round of drafts of the manuscript and helped in the selection of the cover picture. Your positive and critical observations were instrumental in making *The Gift of Job Loss* what it is. I am thankful for having all of you in my life: Sabine Collins, Kesha Dirkson, Sydney Dugan, Susan Erickson, Sara Fox, Suzanne Janel, Lou Kokernak, Samuel C. Li, Dr. Frank Steinmetz, and Doug Wyatt.

Nobody was more involved along the way from book idea to completion than Claudia M. Hausoel, who I had met in a small airplane on the way to the Mayan ruins of Tikal in Guatemala. You, more than anybody else, have been my continuous support and giver of smart advice.

I would also like to express thanks to those who encouraged me to take time off, write this book, or gave me tips on writing—my good friends, esteemed former colleagues, and trustworthy headhunters, respectively: Dr. Maryam Afshar, Gadi Benmark, Dr. Line Bjorge, Paul Bond, Kathleen Bowie (in memoriam), Dr. Wolfgang Hammes, Dr. Karl Henion, Leslie Hecht, Andrea and Oliver Hildenbrand, Kaihan Krippendorf, Sal Magnone, Anne-Marie McGonnigal, Dr. Gunnar Pritsch, Dr. Jakob Rehäuser, Geeta Sankappanavar, Dan Smith, Robyn Stecher, Ruben Trevino, and Chris Vogelgesang.

To my parents I owe eternal gratitude for providing me with the necessary education, love, and discipline to advance in life.

Helping to get my book into a mistake-free manuscript were my editors Sharon Lindenburger and Joanne Sprott. The cover was designed by Lori S. Malkin who had to deal stoically with my layman's input into graphic design.

Lastly, I would like to thank the good people of this wonderful country. The many years I have been in the US have been very rewarding. I am deeply grateful for being here.

ABOUT THE AUTHOR ·····································

MICHAEL A. FROEHLS used his time of job loss after 15 years of a global career to travel, learn, and realize a few things he had always dreamt about.

Michael's professional life began as a management consultant at McKinsey & Company, the preeminent consulting firm. Later he joined Citigroup in New York City as Director of Strategy in the Consumer Bank. After various executive roles including building and running Citi's in-house consulting unit, he was recruited to Allianz Group, one of the largest global multi-line insurance groups, heading global special projects for the CFO and the Executive Committee. His last corporate employer was MetLife, the largest life insurance company in the US. Within its International division Michael was in charge of running Strategic Planning for the 16 countries in which the company had operations outside the US. He is the owner of a boutique consulting and publishing company, The Froehls Group, LLC.

Born in Europe, Michael speaks four languages fluently— English, French, German, and Spanish. He worked in Europe, Canada, Latin America, and for over a decade in the US. He traveled to over 50 countries for business or pleasure, including India, China, and many developing countries.

Michael holds a MBA with distinction from the McCombs School of Business of the University of Texas at Austin, a PhD in Finance from the University of Trier (Germany), and a MA of Industrial Economics from Germany's highly acclaimed business school, the Otto Beisheim School of Corporate Management (WHU Koblenz).

In his free time, Michael enjoys opera and classical music, though has barely time to practice the piano. He is an avid reader, traveler, and fan of Latin America and its many diverse cultures. Michael is a resident of Austin, Texas, one of the best cities to live and work in the United States.

---

*If you want to contact Michael for speaking engagements, consultations, or any other business matter, please send an e-mail to **michael@thegiftofjobloss.com**. If you would like to opine on the book, share your own story for future editions, or just marvel at some amazing pictures from Michael's travel journeys, please go to **www.thegiftofjobloss.com**.*

INDEX ....

LaVergne, TN USA
13 February 2011
216354LV00002B/3/P